FEDERICO GARCÍA LORCA

Poet and Martyr

Matt A. Casado

TABLE OF CONTENTS

Federico García Lorca (1898-1936). Spanish poet, playwright and theater director assassinated in his native Granada by nationalist forces at the beginning of the Spanish Civil War.

PREFACE

I came to write about Federico Garcia Lorca because his image haunts me. For so many years his name was rarely mentioned, his writing forbidden reading, his homosexuality loathed, his death ignored, the place of his burial unknown. It still is. His beloved city, Granada, is just two and a half hours by car from the coastal village where I grew up. Few of us had cars then, though. A trip to the throbbing city of Granada required taking a small lumbering train, often with live chickens and rabbits aboard, or a rickety bus. For the trip my mother would pack *bocadillos de tortilla* (a hefty omelet sandwich), a yank of sausage, almonds, and dried figs from her farm.

At that time, Generalissimo Francisco Franco, having prevailed in Spain's civil war which decimated the nation from 1936 to 1939, was the de facto leader of the country. Much of the western world, following recommendations of President Franklin Roosevelt, joined Americans in boycotting our country hoping the consequent economic pressure would cause the dictatorial government to topple. It didn't. The post-war sanctions did, however, contribute to years of stark poverty that no Spaniard who lived through them can forget.

The dictatorship was aligned with the Catholic church. Although Americans tend to assume Spain's civil war was a struggle between democracy and dictatorship, we Spaniards think of it more as a struggle between anti-religion communism which was on the rise, and Catholicism. As the religion-side of the struggle won, laws which conformed to it were passed. Divorce, homosexuality, licentious books and theater were forbidden. Schools were Catholic schools, all male or all female, national holidays were religious holidays, and the writing of Federico Garcia Lorca, among the best literature in the Spanish language, was prohibited.

I had never heard of Lorca myself until one day in 1953, my anti-Franco father, brought home a precious copy of Lorca's poems permitted to be published for the first time. That is when my father, an anarchist, told me the dramatic and tragic story of the poet's life. If you were not raised in a dictatorship, you might not understand the powerful effect of a government-controlled propaganda machine. In schools, children are taught to abhor political liberty, democracy…and all that goes with it.

Consequently, I did not throw my hat in my father's ring. I believed in our leader, the Generalissimo. However, I was intrigued by the sample of Lorca's poetry I read that day, though the general public wouldn't have access to his entire body of work until much later, when Franco died in 1975 and democracy was reinstated. Here, I would like to add my own small contribution to the story of this outstanding writer in the canon of Spanish literature.

INTRODUCTION

Federico Garcia Lorca. Perhaps no name evokes such a feeling of melancholy, and in the old a shudder of fear, in Spaniards as the name of this 20th century poet who in his brief life reveals the dramatic soul of Spain and whose early death represents the horror of the Spanish Civil War. To understand Garcia Lorca's place in the literary canon of Spain, one must first know a little of the political environment during his time which explodes in the war with an estimated one million Spaniards dead by the end of the fratricide struggle.

By 1898, Spain had lost almost everything, its short-lived hope of joining the democratic movement of Europe, and the remnants of its empire in the Spanish American War. The country lived by usurious foreign loans for which it paid by handing over iron and copper, and pawning railroads to foreign owners. Spain was without industry while large modern industries were developing in Western Europe and North America. Its fertile but mismanaged lands were exhausted while irrigation schemes and new agricultural methods were futilely discussed; in fact, the country was short of bread. The best writers, poets, and thinkers of the period strove to express their haunting experience of defeat to explain and overcome it. They become the leaders of a movement of intellectual and social self-criticism known as the Generation of '98. Later, there was a period from World War I to the late twenties when the young people, Lorca's generation, strove to inspire social and political renovation of Spain. This group of writers and poets came to be known in the Spanish cultural world in 1927, a year of the tribute to the 16th century lyric poet Luis de Góngora, commemorating the third centenary of his death.

Federico García Lorca (according to Spanish custom the first surname is the father's, the second the mother's), was born in the village of Fuente Vaqueros on June 5, 1898. The eldest of four children, his father was a wealthy landowner in the area with workers and servants, so the youngster was immersed in the folklore of the peasants and Gypsies of Granada from birth. They lived in a white house in the center of the village of Fuente Vaqueros some eighteen miles from Granada City. The town had some 2,500 residents and was built over springs flanked by two small rivers. At the age of 10, his family moved to the city where Federico attended a Roman Catholic high school and enrolled afterwards in the University of Granada at the age of 15 to study law, literature and composition, as well as music with Don Antonio Segura who help him become an exceptional pianist.

The young Lorca found inspiration in other artists meeting regularly at the Café Alameda to spend evenings together in conversation. In Granada he was believed to be a homosexual, attracting the hostility that Spanish males meted out to those who fell outside their traditional concept of virility. His early poems reflect a clear sense of isolation and an identification with Granada's rejected groups – Jews, Moors and Gypsies.

Between 1919 and 1925 Lorca's artistic output steadily increased, writing poetry and drama. He led a very intensive life writing many of his well-known poems and plays at that time among which *Gypsy Ballads* (1928), *Blood Wedding,* (1932), *Yerma,* (1934), *Lament for a Bullfighter,* (1935) and *The House of Bernarda Alba,* (1936). Franco's regime banned Lorca's work from his death in 1936 until 1953 when the ban was rescinded. It was then that his poems and plays were published and made known worldwide.

By July 1936 the whole of Spain was in turmoil. The growing political unrest since the beginning of the democratic republic in 1931 came to a head when Franco's troops in Spanish Morocco revolted against the government and invaded the mainland. At the time Lorca was in Granada which quickly came under military rule. Federico was a member of the Generation of 1927, which included writers and poets active in the Spanish cultural world in that year. Other members of the Generation of '27 were the cinematographer Luis Buñuel, the painter Salvador Dalí, and poets like Jorge Guillén, Dámaso Alonso and Rafael Alberti. Many of them supported the democratic republic and opposed the military take-over, a position for which they would eventually go into hiding or be sentenced to exile, prison or death.

This book is a tribute to a writer who explained so well the essence of Andalusia and its peoples. The main intention is to ensure that the remembrance of the poet's work is not forgotten as time passes on. It is an approximation of his work, which is based on the oral traditions of Andalusia, and to his secrets as a man. Lorca was a musician and a performer with total control of his voice and gestures which thrilled those who listened to him. As director of an itinerant group of university student actors called La Barraca, he gave theater freshness and flexibility updating dramas by Calderón, Cervantes and other classic playwrights to show the social struggle people in Spain faced in the 1930's. He brought classical national Spanish theater to the forefront at the time.

As for poetry, Federico dealt with the eternal themes of life: love, joy, sorrow and death. Lorca can be seen as a builder of literary labyrinths taken from deep Andalusian folk tales. During his childhood years of contact with people of the countryside in Granada he was able to immerse himself in their popular customs and sayings that are reflected in his poems, lullabies, children's songs, and farmers' refrains. He used his own metaphors such as scenes in people's eyes and references to the omnipresent moon. And in spite of his focus on Andalusian folklore, his poetry became paradoxically universal.

His work shows his ability to identify with the inner world of women. His intimate relationship with his mother and sisters remained throughout his life. An old family servant, a peasant woman named Dolores, left her mark on his imagination and understanding of country people by teaching him folk legends, popular figures of speech and folk songs to whose rhythm he is said to have responded even before he could speak.

Federico felt so deeply the essence of the Moorish Andalusian land that his spirit merged with the scenery making nature the echo of his heart. He emphasized his Andalusian universe describing Córdoba as a nostalgic, melancholic and silent city and its people as dramatic and taciturn. Seville, on the contrary, is seen by Lorca as a joyful city, as a brilliant jewel with its Moorish Giralda bell tower piercing the sky. But his view of Granada is essential for understanding the poet. He was always loyal to the city, a place where he felt himself at home, where he could relax and work in peace although he was nostalgic for old Granada that had lost its great Arab civilization, with its own astronomy, architecture and poetry. He was proud of the remaining beautiful Alhambra palace with its unique arabesques and secluded myrtle gardens with delicate fountains.

Lorca's work spoke of horses and wild bulls as part of the Andalusian essence. He liked bullfighting and thought of it as pure drama in which one sees death surrounded by beauty. He couldn't imagine spring in Spain without the dramatic sound of bugles in its sunny bullrings and the deadly struggle between a majestic animal and an elegant matador.

Federico uses premonition of his death through the protagonists of his poems. His tragic theater is an exaltation of death itself. It is a dramatic battle between red, warm blood and the agony of the dying man, often witnessed from above by a cold, pale moon. In Lorca's world, moon and blood are a mirror of life and death where life is human and burning and death is mechanical and cold. His rural tragedies strip away the masks behind which his characters attempt to conceal their true nature. Federico García Lorca was an extremely Spanish writer who presented the image of his country evoking the Gypsies of Andalusia, the bullfight, life in sun baked villages and the powerful forces of passion and honor.

While his work is profoundly and revealingly Spanish, at the same time it is universally human. He saw the suffering and joy, beauty and terror, love and death of mankind. The emotional forces he released became part of the shapeless revolutionary movements of Spain whether he intended it or not. For this, it was inevitable that Lorca be martyred by fascist brutality, his work becoming a liberal banner. When news of his death become known to the people, some of whom could not read or write, they learned his ballads by heart. Tunes of the simple folk songs he had revived became war songs of the fighting Republicans.

PART 1

The Beginning

El lagarto está llorando.	Mr. lizard is crying.
La lagarta está llorando.	Mrs. lizard is crying.
El lagarto y la lagarta	Mr. and Mrs. lizard
con delantalitos blancos	wearing little white aprons.

CHAPTER 1

FUENTE VAQUEROS – 1898

In the last decade of the nineteenth century, Fuente Vaqueros was a small town in the Vega of Granada. A *vega* is a watered, fertile plain usually divided into agricultural smallholdings where cereals and vegetables grow together with fruit trees cultivated in groves. The village, located some 18 miles west of the city of Granada, is separated from the Mediterranean by the imposing mountain chain of Sierra Nevada where the highest peak on the peninsula soars to an altitude of 11,400 feet. The Vega of Granada was first settled by the Arabs who invaded Spain in 711 A.D. and used an elaborate system of ditches and irrigation channels to water the arable land. Many of these first settlers were asked to leave the area in 1609 after being expulsed by Spanish King Felipe III, but many remained after being forced to convert to the Catholic faith. The conquerors divided the land into small holdings which were owned by Spanish families for generations. Most of the laborers were those Arabs farmers who stayed after converting to

Christianity. Those families conserved their forefathers' traditions and idiosyncrasies which would come to have such a great influence on Federico.

By the end of the 1880's, the cultivation of sugar-beet was introduced successfully in the area creating much activity, including the building of beet-processing factories. With the loss of Cuba to the United States in 1898 and the consequent end of cheap sugar importation, the importance of the industry in the Vega became paramount. Most landowners made enormous gains, among them Federico García Rodríguez, father of García Lorca. In fact, Don Federico became one of the wealthiest landowners in the village.

The four brothers García Rodríguez of Fuente Vaqueros had a long ancestry in the town. Their father Enrique, secretary of the town hall, named his first son Federico after his brother, who was a renowned guitar player. Lorca's father was born in 1859 to become a serious and determined individual from whom the poet would inherit his wide forehead and thick eyebrows. In 1880 Don Federico married Matilde Palacios who unexpectedly died fourteen years later unable to have children. The story of being barren greatly impacted impressionable young Federico and that was undoubtedly the background for his play *Yerma* (Barren).

On August 27, 1897, at the age of thirty-seven, Don Federico remarried a soft-spoken young woman named Vicenta Lorca Romero, a quiet, serious local school mistress, daughter of an agricultural worker. The poet believed that he inherited Jewish blood from her, his mother. Vicenta's family was poor and her early years were hard. She was obliged to board at a charity school run by nuns for the education of poor girls. Vicenta used to tell her children about her unhappy years at the school. The poet would later recount his mother's bad experiences in the unfinished play *The Dreams of My Cousin Aurelia.* In 1892, Vicenta graduated as an elementary school teacher from the Women Teachers' Training College at Granada. Her first job was in an elementary school for girls in Fuente Vaqueros where she met and married the widowed Federico García Rodríguez.

On June 5, 1898, Vicenta gave birth to the poet who was soon baptized and named Federico del Santo Corazón de Jesús García Lorca. He was born in the farmhouse built by his father in 1880 upon his first marriage. His mother, not being well at the time and unable to breastfeed, entrusted the task of breastfeeding the baby to a wetnurse, the wife of one of Don Federico's employees who lived nearby. When he was two years old, his mother gave birth to a second child but twenty months later the baby died of pneumonia. Witnessing that, Federico learned that life and death are two halves of an undecipherable whole.

As a young child, playing outdoors with his friends, Lorca developed a genuine love of nature. He had several cousins in Fuente Vaqueros, some of them older. Aurelia was one of his favorites whom he visited frequently. She was the protagonist on the play *The Dreams of My Cousin Aurelia.* Another favorite was Clotilde, the daughter of his uncle Francisco, but the person that molded his artistic nature was his mother, Vicenta. It was from her that Federico developed his love for reading and the arts, and his religious fervor. He used to accompany his mother to the chapel to attend mass and to watch the pious processions in town organized by the church.

There were many factors that affected Federico's Andalusian bent. As a child, he was absorbing into his poet's mind and his dramatist's imagination details of the way the Vega looked and the turns of local peasants' speech as they discussed people and life. Three other elements of the Vega stayed with him and were later fashioned into literary fame. The first was the *duende,* a hidden spirit that people or things may have, one of the roots of the gypsy soul. The second was puppet shows of travelling troupes performing in Fuente Vaqueros that fascinated him. He would go on to write puppet plays presented by the itinerant University Theater in 1932. Also, he was entranced by stories told evenings by the hearth by Salvador, an older worker of Don Federico's, about Gypsies, ghosts, goblins, wolves, woods, death, and enchanted characters in common folk stories. Years after the death of Salvador, Federico vividly remembered his stories and absorbed them into his literary work. His interests as a young child were puppets and music and his favorite game was saying mass and giving the sermon. The third element of the Vega was the *Guardia Civil* (Civil Guard), the federal police, that in Federico's mind took on the guise of evil itself. Later on, he wrote a ballad that made the Guards infamous describing them as being a heartless power.

The García household was moved in 1907 by Don Federico from Fuente Vaqueros to the town of Asquerosa where he had bought a large estate. He came to own two homes in the village, a farm on the edge of town and a large two-story house in the center, a lavish residence by village standards with stables, a corral, four bedrooms, a kitchen, a dining room, and an imposing pair of lightning rods on the roof. To Federico, it was a dramatic change that revealed to him the cloistered, provincial nature of life in a tiny rural community.

At the age of ten, his parents abruptly sent Federico to school in Almería, a Mediterranean seaport nearly a hundred miles to the southeast, to prepare him for his entrance examination to secondary school under the tutelage of their good friend Antonio Rodríguez, the former schoolmaster of Fuente Vaqueros. Don Federico and Vicenta admired their friend's pragmatism and devotion to work, as well as his liberal outlook and quiet anticlericalism. The boy having never been separated from his parents or the Vega, felt estranged from other children. In school, he was an indifferent student who distinguished himself by coning puns and clever nicknaming for his classmates. However, Federico managed to complete his schoolwork and pass his entrance exam for the Technical Institute in Almería which he did attend, but after a few months he felt ill of a gum infection and had to return home to recover. His parents decided not to send Federico back to Almería and instead enroll him in the Technical Institute in Granada. In the summer of 1909, the family moved to the city where Don Federico rented a three-story house.

Federico's childhood in the Vega had ended; it was now time for him and his younger brother Francisco to study for a professional career. As is usually the case, the two brothers were very different: Federico, absorbed in observation, enchanted and tormented by life around him; Francisco, tangible and solid. The poet's early recollections of his first years in Fuente Vaqueros were those of learning how to read and play music with his mother, and the awareness of social injustice towards the poor.

CHAPTER 2
GRANADA – 1909

At the start of the twentieth century, Granada was an inconspicuous capital in the southern Spanish region of Andalusia. It was an isolated town provincial in its society, but laden with traditions from ancient Roman Andalusia through the intricate civilizations of the Moors to the flowering of the Spanish Renaissance and the long slow decline of later centuries. The population included a dominant white class, descendants of the conquerors of the Arab kingdom in 1492, a large population of converted Moors, plus 20,000 Sephardic Jews, and a myriad of Gypsies living in caves in the nearby hills of the Sacromonte. Although all professed the Catholic faith, all retained their own customs and idiosyncrasies. Federico made friends with the Gypsies, most of them dancers and singers, later describing their exotic language and behavior in his work *Gypsy Ballads.*

The city was being modernized with the profits from sugar production in the province, and old emblematic, historic buildings erected by the Moors and early Christians were being replaced by state-of-the-art constructions. While its sister provincial city of Seville in the east of Andalusia had prospered since the discovery of America because of its access to the sea, Granada, cut off from the coast by the lofty Sierra Nevada chain, had remained economically a rather backward enclave. Federico made frequent visits to the city's most celebrated monument, the Alhambra, which sits high above town on a steep hill covered with sycamores and cypress trees. From this height, Arab kings presided in luxury over the final two centuries of Muslim rule in Spain. Their reign ended under the rule of Isabel and Ferdinand in 1492, when Catholic armies swept into Granada and toppled the fabled kingdom. Soon thereafter, both Arabs and Jews became disadvantaged minorities, subject to prejudicial racial laws. Throughout his life, Lorca voiced his support for the persecuted and talked of the endless duel between the Arab and Christian cultures.

Granada with the Alhambra palace in the forefront and
the snowy peaks of Sierra Nevada in the background.

The new large García-Lorca house in Granada included a patio with a small fountain, a garden with several varieties of flowers, a stable and servants from the Vega who enriched the imagination of the poet with their distinct speech, songs and tales. Two of the women that moved to Granada with the García's were Aunt Isabel and Dolores Cuesta who had also been the wetnurse of the poet's brother Francisco in Fuente Vaqueros. Both became mother substitutes when Vicenta was absent from the household and greatly influenced the life of the poet as a young man. Isabel taught him to play the guitar to accompany the folk songs sung by Dolores that he would later reproduce in his literary works.

Although the nearby Arab Alhambra palace was almost in ruins at the time, since the middle of the nineteenth century it had attracted a plethora of sightseer and foreign writers. It was first rediscovered by French romantic playwriters Chateaubriand and Victor Hugo and soon afterwards by Washington Irving who wrote his well-known *Tales of the Alhambra*. There were also foreign composers inspired by the uniqueness of the site. Russian musician Mijaíl Glinka spent several months in 1845 in the city where he was introduced to the *cante jondo,* or songs of the Gypsies, which would also later influence the poetry of Federico. Claude Debussy wrote several musical works after listening to the songs of a group of Andalusian Gypsies. Federico would play Debussy's music which he thought reverberated the essence of the enchanting Alhambra.

Federico and Francisco García Lorca were enrolled in the College of the Sacred Heart of Jesus, a secular private school where they studied towards their high school diploma. The younger brother was a good student while Federico could not concentrate well on his lessons; he was a shy, distracted pupil seating in the back row more interested in drawing than in learning his academic lessons; he would rather spend hours playing piano at home than finish his homework. The only teacher he liked was his private music instructor Antonio Segura whom he revered. He stimulated Federico's innate musical talent and taught him harmony. At age sixteen Federico gave a concert at his school and his playing of Beethoven sonatas so impressed the president of the institution that he took the promising youngster under his wing.

In 1914, shortly before graduating, the poet's father compelled the brothers to pursue a career at the University of Granada. After passing a year of preparatory courses common to both letters and law, Federico enrolled in the then lackluster program of letters. Two of the university professors greatly influenced the higher education of the poet. Martín Domínguez Berrueta, chair of the theory of literature and the arts department, who organized study trips around the country, stimulated Federico's interest in the Arts, and Fernando de los Ríos, who came to the University of Granada from the Free Teaching Institute in Madrid. De los Ríos regarded himself as a spiritual grandson of the eminent educator Giner de los Ríos, a distant relative who founded the unorthodox school in Madrid. Don Fernando believed that after the disastrous defeat by the United States in Cuba and the Philippines, Spain needed a cultural reformation. His influence on the poet's liberal views was crucial for the poet.

In May 1916, Segura died which left Federico without his support in convincing his father to allow him to study music in Paris. Don Federico refused, so his son turned his creative energy to poetry. Federico had met the poet Antonio

Fernando de los Ríos Urruti (1879-1949). Socialist politician,
professor of law and mentor to Federico García Lorca.

Machado on a school trip to Baeza, where he was a teacher.
He attended a lecture where Machado discussed his book
of poems, *Fields of Castile,* and recited some verses by the
Nicaraguan poet Rubén Darío. Federico was enthralled.
Don Antonio exemplified Lorca's idea of a writer resist-
ing both artistic and intellectual fads, influenced by mod-
ernism but withstanding its decadent excesses. He taught
Federico to regard poetry as a melancholy medium and to
view the poet's mission as a solitary one.

In Baeza, the poet met Lorenzo Martinez Fuset who
was also studying in Granada. They became close friends
and established a close relationship that lasted for years. In

October of 1916 Berrueta organized a 21-day student trip through Castile and Galicia with stops in Madrid, Ávila, Burgos and Salamanca. This contact with other parts of Spain greatly influenced Federico who later reflected on his experiences in his work *Impressions and Landscapes*. During this trip, Federico felt that, besides his music, he had a literary vocation. The first result of that realization was a short piece of poetic prose titled *Symbolic Fantasy* published in 1917 in the Granada Arts Club's bulletin. In this work, the author asserted the romantic nature of Granada with its exotic Moorish past. His early writings were a beginner's passionate efforts to find a subject and a voice.

Federico had joined the Center of Arts and Literature in 1915 that was presided over by Fernando de los Ríos who would take an active interest in Federico's development and influenced the course of his life at several turning points. The writers of the center's magazine entitled *Granada* were several young men who intended to represent the ideals of their generation. The authors of the publication met each evening at the back of the Café Alameda in a recess they called El Rinconcillo (The Little Corner). Federico was a member and met several others who became life-long friends. Now interested in religion, the poet wrote several articles in which he seemed to believe that Christ's example and sacrifice had been useless and that a share of the blame must fall on the shoulders of the official representatives of Jesus on earth, starting with the Pope. The dislike of those clergy he regarded as celibate hypocrites was evident.

Federico also loathed militarism at a time of the bloody fighting in World War I in Europe and in the Spanish Protectorate in Morocco. He wrote an essay in 1917 lashing out against those who enticed young men with false notions of patriotism. He detested the alliance of sword and cross and the adulation of the national flag. In his opinion, the name of Jesus was used for negative nationalistic purposes and that had given rise to innumerable atrocities. Instead, the nation should produce citizens who are lovers of peace and know the real message of the Gospel. Don Federico blamed the reunions at El Rinconcillo for Lorca's growing delinquency at school, but for the poet it was the first set of friends since childhood with whom he had felt a genuine affinity and he spent as much time with them as he could.

Domínguez Berrueta's class made a last trip through Castilian lands with a prolonged stay in the city of Burgos. Federico's first book, *Impressions and Landscapes,* grew out of these excursions. The work, printed in 1918, describe the author's contemplations on his study trips to Castile, Baeza and from his Granada. The book received two local reviews, one hailing its skill and sincerity, the other calling it a portrait of the author, with his desires, dislikes, aspirations and dreams of arts and poetry. At twenty, Federico proved himself to be an incipient, talented modernist writer. In the prologue Lorca wrote that reality is worthless without considering our sentiments and that there is poetry in everything be it pretty, ugly or even repugnant although the difficulty is in knowing how to discover it. His vision of the cities he visited was melancholic. He observed the grave peal of bells and the mysticism of churches and cathedrals. The first part of the book corresponds to the notes the poet took when visiting cities and towns and uses his colorful prose to describe Granada, writing descriptive and metaphorical passages about the sounds and hues of the city. The work also contains romantic evocations of the gardens of convents, churches and private houses of Granada, a city where Federico was considered to be a homosexual in a place noted for its aversion towards unconventional sexuality. Although the poet returned to Granada as often as he could, he increasingly found the people of Granada apathetic and reactionary. Federico himself considered his first book mediocre though after its publication he gave copies to friends and acquaintances.

At the university, Federico could study subjects like history of art, literature or elementary concepts of philosophy but failure was inevitable in subjects requiring greater effort and discipline. He got as far as the final examination in historical grammar but went down in failure. Lorca's increasing difficulties in the School of Letters and the lack of serious pressure from his family, resulted in his being an average student for a few years, and then trying his fortune in the School of Law, where he passed a few easy subjects.

CHAPTER 3

MADRID – 1919

In 1919 Lorca was twenty-one years old. Equipped with several letters of introduction and a set of new clothes, he set off for the capital in the spring. Fernando de los Ríos had persuaded Don Federico that his son should continue his education in Madrid where he could live and learn in the free atmosphere of the Residencia de Estudiantes. Lorca registered himself in the Residence, an offspring of the Free Teaching Institution founded in 1876 by Francisco Giner de los Ríos. There he stayed until 1928 whenever he was not back in Granada. The school was run by Alberto Jiménez Fraud who followed the directives of Giner in the preparation of a select minority of cultured individuals devoted to the advancement of liberal ideas in the country. The aim of the residential college was to expand the outlook of its students by bridging the gap between the sciences and the humanities. The rector and his teaching staff strived to create a group of students who believed in the cause of a new Spain and to empower them with critical thinking skills so they would not blindly adopt the opinions of others.

The purpose of the school was supported by intellectuals like philosophers Miguel de Unamuno and José Ortega y Gasset. In view of its success, the demand for rooms increased and the college board decided to build a larger residence for 150 students in the outskirts of the city with views to the north of the Guadarrama mountains. Many dignitaries lectured at the Residence, including Albert Einstein, Francois Mauriac and John Maynard Keynes. There were renowned foreign and national musicians, among them Igor Stravinsky, Manuel de Falla and Rodolfo Halfter, invited to speak as composers and performers.

Federico joined the Residence where other students, friends from Granada, already awaited his arrival. He checked in with a letter of introduction to poet Juan Ramón Jiménez from Fernando de los Ríos. Juan Ramón decided to help the very enthusiastic new student. The poet soon befriended the future film director Luis Buñuel who had the reputation of being one of the most original characters staying at the school. Appalled when he learned of the rumor that Lorca was homosexual, he approached the poet and demanded verification. Lorca didn't answer the question but his homosexuality was soon apparent.

Meanwhile, Federico had already taken his first steps in theater and in poetry and was beginning to be known beyond Granada when he decided to finish his studies in law. He had already passed a few subjects but over half of his coursework remained. After barely passing several courses, only mercantile law stood between him and the degree. Federico finally would pass the exam in 1923.

In March of 1920, his play *The Butterfly's Evil Spell* was staged in the Eslava Theater in Madrid. Federico introduced the work from the stage as humble but disturbing. A moment later the curtain rose on a green meadow peopled by actors wearing dark capes meant to resemble cockroach' shells. The characters, despite their insect nature, were meant to acquire human dimensions and passions with which the public attending could identify. Unfortunately, the audience rejected it and Federico's first dramatic work was a fiasco. At the time, the public was accustomed to plays such as those by conventional playwright Jacinto Benavente and to the amusing romantic comedies by the Quintero brothers. It was obvious that a section of the audience was determined to sink the show, shouting deafening catcalls and insults together with foot-stampings and boos. By the end it was clear that Madrid was not ready for a play about the amorous misfortunes of cockroaches. The press referred to the failure of the play with none of the critics writing of the ironic elements of the work and others rejecting the idea that cockroaches could be protagonists of a play. Although the work was interesting in many ways it only lasted four performances. Lorca took the failure well and even laughed about the disastrous evening. Federico's father now pressed the poet to leave his writing and apply himself to get a university degree as his brother Francisco had done. In response, Federico resumed his studies in Granada. After passing Spanish literature and world history, his father let him return to Madrid on the condition that he continue his higher education studies.

Installed again at the Residence, Lorca told his parents about writing poetry and of having a book published. His mother Vicenta approved of his determination to have a literary career, adding in a letter that she 'was praying to the Virgin that everything worked out well and that he not be upset for any reason.'

His work *Book of Poems* was printed in June 1921 with a dedication to his brother Francisco. The book was the poet's recollection of his days of youth and adolescence. One critic remarked that the poems were too sentimental which in his view marred much of the work but that Lorca would eventually become a genuine poet of the avant-garde. Federico commented that if in the book he had not yet found himself, he felt that he was on the right path 'full of daisies and multicolored lizards.' In fact, the author showed in this formative stage of his career that his writings were gaining maturity with beautiful lyric passages. In this work, Lorca manages to create his own poetry without losing contact with the traditional. Sensual and elegiac, *Book of Poems* turned out to be a work of a gifted although immature writer.

In the summer of 1921, Lorca took guitar lesson with two Gypsies who played and sang with popular appeal. Convinced that true *cante jondo* (deep song) had been supplanted by flamenco played to tourists in gaudy revues, Lorca sought to hear *cante jondo* in its original state. It was a new interest in this folk music of Andalusia in purest form that was to lead to his *Poem of Cante Jondo* and *Gypsy Ballads*. At the same time, Lorca also began to write a puppet play that would be the point of departure for *The Tragicomedy of Don Cristóbal and Señorita Rosita*.

By then, Lorca surely felt optimistic about his literary vocation but, unfortunately, he had totally neglected his university studies. From this moment on the poet never again tried to complete his BA courses although he still wanted to finish his law degree.

When in Granada, Lorca became a frequent visitor to Manuel de Falla's *carmen* (a secluded villa enclosed by gardens) on the slopes of the Alhambra, with a splendid view of both Sierra Nevada and the city, where the composer came to regard him with paternal affection, praising his many gifts and his piano expertise. Don Manuel proposed to stage a *cante jondo* competition in Granada, a festival of national scope and importance that would illuminate the distinction between true deep song and its poor cousin flamenco in which musicians from throughout Andalusia could participate. The organizers envisioned the festival as a matter of national as well as international significance, an occasion whereby Spain could pay formal tribute to the country's rich musical heritage. The event was scheduled to take place in the Alhambra during the Corpus Christi celebration.

Lorca became deeply involved and wrote a series of poems for the contest. The work, full of Gypsies, oil lamps, and forges, was entitled *Poem of Cante Jondo*. It includes death, unhappy love and despair embellished by the author's innate image-making capacity. He believed that the passion of this primitive music expressed the depths of the Andalusian soul, explaining the *cante jondo* as a rare example of primitive song, one of the oldest in all Europe. To the Gypsies this deep song is a folk art handed down in all its complexity from generation to generation. Lorca attributed the development of deep song to be the blend liturgical song of the Spanish Catholic Church, the musical tradition that came with the Moorish invasion of Spain and to the arrival of numerous bands of Gypsies in the area. After the festival was over, Federico declared that no two people were better equipped to supervise it than a musician like the great maestro, Manuel de Falla, and a poet like himself.

In the summer of 1922, Lorca finished the first draft of the tragic comedy of *Don Cristóbal and Señorita Rosita*. He wrote excitedly to Falla who agreed to write the music for the puppet play. It was a considerable improvement over *The Butterfly's Evil Spell* for Lorca had now found his authentic voice as a dramatist. The play included dialogues modelled on the speech habits of the people of the Vega and the theme of society's suppression of individual liberty. Meanwhile, Lorca tried to make one last effort to finish his university degree.

Finally, after nine long years, Federico completed his law degree in February of 1923, although he never again mentioned his university career. His father allowed him to return to the Residence in Madrid after an absence of a year and a half, this time accompanied by his brother Francisco who was ready to begin studying for his doctorate. At the Residence, Lorca met Salvador Dalí who was to have a profound influence in his life. Born in Catalonia, the eighteen-year-old Dalí wore his hair very long and liked to dress extravagantly. He was an admirer of the painter Juan Gris and was beginning to experiment with cubism under his influence. The Catalan thought of himself as a prodigy, destined to be the savior of contemporary painting. Salvador was accepted at the school by the other students and soon became a man-about-town frequenting the poshest bars in Madrid. Lorca was immediately attracted by the looks, personality and talent of the painter and Dalí by the charism and genius of the poet. From the start, Salvador Dalí, Luis Buñuel and Lorca became close friends with Federico being the center of attention in literary or any other social gatherings.

At the beginning of 1923, Lorca started work on a comic opera, *Lola the Stage Actress,* a bittersweet love story set in rural Andalusia, with music by Manuel de Falla. The work was never completed because the composer, a staunch Catholic, may have had doubts about its morality.

In the fall Federico got the idea of writing a play about Mariana Pineda, an Andalusian heroine who was executed in 1831 for having embroidered a flag for the liberal revolutionaries fighting against the repressive rule of King Fernando VII. For Lorca, Pineda became a martyr for liberty. A statue of Mariana, a symbol of revolutionary ideal, stood in a square below his bedroom in Granada and as a young man, he had stared so often at her gray stone presence that he felt compelled to exalt her. Federico aimed to depict Pineda as he believed she was in reality. Instead of writing about the Mariana Pineda of history, the sensual lover and courageous activist executed for her political ideals, he would present the Mariana of legend, the romantic heroine of the tales and ballads he had heard as a child. After the play was finished, it took four years to have it produced, when Lorca was already considered a great talent among contemporary Spanish poets.

In the summer of 1924, Federico turned his attention to the completion of his *Gipsy Ballads* which started with the *Ballad of the Moon Moon,* written the previous year, to be followed by other poems like *Ballad of Black Anguish* and *Ballad of the Spanish Civil Guard.* In this work he intended to reflect the essence of Andalusia using the Gypsies as a refrain. It was a monumental project where the author wanted to include, in his own words, 'Gypsies, horses, archangels, planets, its Jewish and Roman bents, rivers, crimes, the everyday touch of the smuggler and the celestial touch of the naked children of Cordova who tease Saint Raphael, patron saint of the city.' At the same time the work would be anti-picturesque, anti-folkloric, and anti-flamenco. A formidable task. The traditional struggle between the Gypsies and the Civil Guard, the rural paramilitary institution founded in 1842 to put down banditry, was well known in Spain, particularly in Andalusia where the frequent bloody encounters were notorious.

The poems of the *Gypsy Ballads* were written between 1924 and 1927. But during the summer of 1924, Federico had already started working on *The Shoemaker's Prodigious Wife.* The play would be in the puppet tradition enlivened with flute and guitar music. The theme involves an elderly man married to a young, attractive woman. Federico used some elements from his own background, such as the green dress in which the shoemaker's wife appears at the beginning of the play is like one belonging to Lorca's cousin Clotilde in Fuente Vaqueros. The music performed in the street with flute and guitar used to be played on a clarinet by a musician the author had met. The mayor is related to a character Federico knew when he was a young man in his own village. The bad language of the prodigious wife was comparable to that of Dolores, the Lorca household servant who exploded in rage when she was irritated by her suitor. Because of its literary harmony, this play was to be one of the poet's most successful works. In it, the author connects again with the traditions of the Andalusia which he knew so well since childhood, including the vernacular language of the Vega. In the fall of 1924, Federico returned to Madrid to learn that the production of the work had been postponed.

At the Residence he resumed his friendship with Salvador Dalí and met a young author who was working on a poem book to be titled *Mariner Ashore*. That poet, Rafael Alberti, would become a close friend of Federico.

In January of the following year, Luis Buñuel left the Residence for Paris while Lorca was in Granada finishing the manuscript of *Mariana Pineda*. He ended depicting Mariana as a woman in love who had taken the risk of embroidering the liberal flag in order to please her husband, Manuel. The play ends with the heroine accepting her fate and refusing to scape death by naming the conspirators.

CHAPTER 4
CADAQUÉS – 1925

In April of 1925, Federico accepted an invitation to give a poetry recital in Barcelona and, taking advantage of the occasion, visited Salvador Dalí in Cadaqués, a fishing village in Catalonia's Costa Brava. He was welcomed by the painter, his father and his sister Ana Maria. The Dalí villa was located on the seafront, close to the Mediterranean. The house stood almost alone, its façade reflecting in the sea. Federico fell in love with the seaside village and claimed that the surrounding landscape was eternal and perfect. When Federico read *Mariana Pineda* to the Dalí's and a group of friends, Ana María cried at the end of the recital while her father showed his enthusiasm declaring Lorca to be the greatest poet of the century.

As a group, they took a boat trip to Cape Creus where the Pyrenees end on the coast that Dalí enjoyed painting regularly. Federico was impressed by the large rock formations of the rugged promontory. The two friends enjoyed the traditional festivities of Holy Week in the village and took part in the local processions. Afterwards they traveled to Gerona, capital of the province where they attended mass in its Romanesque cathedral. Lorca commented that nothing could be more beautiful than that region of Spain, except for the Vega in Granada.

Being aware of Federico's obsessive fear of death, it occurred to Dalí to paint Lorca as a corpse. He took sketches of Federico in a recumbent pose and began working on the painting finishing it in 1926. Titled *Still Life* the painting was included in Dalí's exhibition in Barcelona at the end of that year. It was the first of his paintings and drawings in which Lorca appeared. Federico liked Barcelona calling it 'a small Paris' and was busy there giving informal readings of *Mariana Pineda* and of other poems at the Athenaeum.

Also, in April at the Residence, the French poet Louis Aragon gave a lecture on surrealism, an avant-garde movement initiated in France around 1920 by writer and poet André Breton. Lorca did not attend the lecture but was aware of the new cultural tendency from Breton's *Manifesto of Surrealism* that rejects the sterility of modern rationalism.

That summer, Dalí returned to Cadaqués and Federico to Granada. The poet had already written several prose dialogues that he catalogued as pure poetry, feeling that they were more universal, by which he meant less recognizably Andalusian.

Since his visit to Cadaqués, Lorca's feelings for Dalí had grown more intense and his staying in Granada had become intolerable. Now he wanted to leave Spain that was under the strict dictatorship of General Primo de

Rivera. Perhaps he could become a teacher of Spanish abroad. Also, at the age of twenty-seven he was still financially dependent on his parents. Federico confessed to a friend that he was extremely depressed and felt that his literary career and his love-life were collapsing around him. Perhaps the main cause of his depression was his feelings for Dalí. At the end of the summer, Lorca accompanied his family to the Málaga he loved, and there he felt much better.

In November of 1925, Dalí opened an exhibition of seventeen paintings and five drawings in Barcelona with resounding success. This news increased the poet's longing to leave his parent's home and see Salvador but being still financially dependent of his family, there was nothing he could do but to remain in Granada.

With the arrival of a new year, Federico was still desperate to escape from Granada perhaps to join his brother in Toulouse. Francisco had graduated and was working now on his law doctorate in France. His academic success made his parents proud, contrasting with Federico's inability to have his work staged or even published. And yet, the situation didn't make Lorca jealous of his brother but respectful of his achievements. He, himself, had finished *The Love of Don Perlimplín and Belisa in His Garden* which would be one of Lorca's masterpieces as an exploration of sexual impotence in the relationship of an old man married to a younger woman. The plot enabled him to explore a favorite and familiar theme: the conflict between spiritual and sensual love.

Meanwhile, his other plays had not yet been produced and Lorca now felt more than ever that he should escape from Spain. In February, he gave the inaugural address at the new Athenaeum in Granada which he entitled *The Poetic Imagery in Don Luis de Góngora*, a sixteenth century poet whom he considered to be the father of modern poetry. In his lecture, Lorca spoke of his admiration for Góngora's original mode of linguistic expression and use of the metaphor that Federico used in his own work. In fact, he had found pleasing facets of the writing of this author of *Soledades*. At the time, he had almost finished an ode in honor of Salvador Dalí that would be published in April in *Revista de Occidente*, one of the best journals in Europe. The ode was a poetization of surrealistic ideas and an affirmation of Lorca's friendship and admiration for the painter and his work.

In the middle of March, the poet left home and settled once again in the Residencia in Madrid and, the following month, travelled to Valladolid to give a poetry reading at the Arts Club. He was introduced to the audience as a great new poet about to step into the pages of history. The address was a great success, with Lorca reading poems from his three upcoming books and extracts from his *Ode to Salvador Dalí*, a work of twenty-eight stanzas. The poet used provocative metaphors combined with traditional metrics to give the ode a startling sense of newness.

It was in May that Dalí returned to Madrid after a year's absence. Federico was in love with him and tried to initiate an intimate relationship without success as Dalí had no intention of cooperating. In June, Salvador refused to be examined by the Academy which he declared incompetent to sit in judgment of his genius although, in reality, he wanted to sever ties with the School of Fine Arts and continue his studies in Paris.

During the summer, Lorca spent some time in Lanjarón, a spa in the lower Alpujarras mountains south of Granada. He continued work on *Gypsy Ballads* hoping to finish the book while still not having any luck in the production of *Mariana Pineda*. In September, his parents saw nothing practical in his literary endeavors and, again, Federico contemplated the idea of obtaining an academic career in literature but he wasn't sure of how to do it. He moved to a property that his father had recently bought outside Granada which had a farmhouse surrounded by orchards and gardens. Don Federico named it Huerta de San Vicente in honor of his wife Vicenta. From the balcony of the house, Lorca could see both the Vega and the towering Sierra Nevada in the distance, a view he considered the most beautiful panorama of mountains in Europe.

At that time, Dalí in Cadaqués was absorbed in painting a picture of the martyrdom of Saint Sebastian. He and the poet were interested in the iconography of the saint, his manly figure and his passive response to the arrows piercing his flesh. Lorca prepared material for a lecture on *The Myth of St. Sebastian.* In September he asked his friend Jorge Guillén in Valladolid for a photograph of the martyr's 16th century sculpture done by Alonso González de Berruguete preserved in the city's museum.

After Lorca told Jorge his decision to become a literary professor Guillén persuaded their mutual friend Pedro Salinas to look into the possibility of a teaching position for the poet in France. Salinas quickly answered that the true career of Federico was that of being a poet. When Lorca also notified Dalí of his decision to become a teacher of literature, the painter was also horrified and advised Federico to tell his father about the futility of such an endeavor; after all, Lorca was to produce works that would make him famous and economically independent.

A few weeks afterwards Federico abandoned his plans for a university career. At that time, he learned of her sister Concha's engagement to his friend Manuel Fernández-Montesinos, a medical student and former member of El Rinconcillo. The news jolted him and now he suddenly yearned for a conventional life and for the respectability of marriage and fatherhood. But the events of the last two years pointed in a different direction.

In October a new Granada Arts Club opened its 1926-27 session. The poet delivered the inaugural lecture and at that time Emilio Prados, a publisher and friend from Málaga, suggested that Lorca allow him to print his already finished poems. The following month, Prados published the first volume of a new literary magazine, *Litoral,* containing three of Lorca's *Gypsy Ballads.* The work *Songs* appeared the following year. It seemed that Lorca's luck was beginning to turn for the better.

Margarita Xirgu, a leading actress at the time, read the manuscript of *Mariana Pineda* and agreed to present the play at the end of her current season. Federico went to Madrid in March to meet with Xirgu and read his drama to her company. Federico was now sensing that 1927 would be his year of breakthrough.

La ilustre actriz Margarita Xirgu, que ha celebrado brillantemente
su beneficio en el Teatro Eslava con su genial
creación «Zaza»

Margarita Xirgu Subirá (1888-1969). Popular Spanish
stage actress, friend of Federico García Lorca.

PART 2

Breakthrough

El canto quiere ser luz.　The song wants to be light.
En lo oscuro el canto tiene,　In the dark the song shows,
hilos de fósforo y luna.　threads of phosphorous and moon.

CHAPTER 5
MARÍA PINEDA – 1927

In 1923, Lorca had begun work on the play *Mariana Pineda,* a Spanish heroine in the fight against authoritarianism, which would be produced first in Barcelona four years later by actress Margarita Xirgu. Mariana was born in Granada in 1804 and at the age of fifteen married Manuel Peralta, a young man of liberal ideas who died three years later leaving her with two children. Pineda followed her husband's political ideology helping those who were persecuted and jailed during the repression of King Ferdinand VII. In 1828 Mariana helped a liberal military captain escape from prison by smuggling in a friar's robes to disguise him. In a search of her house, the police found a flag on which Mariana had embroidered the slogan 'Equality, Freedom, Law.' She was arrested accused of conspiracy and asked who her accomplices were in exchange for leniency, she refused to reveal them. Consequently, Pineda was executed on May 26, 1831 at the age of 27 with her flag burning in front of her.

Mariana Pineda y Muñoz (1804-1831). Spanish liberal portrayed by Federico García Lorca in a play of the same name, written between 1923 and 1925, based on the life of the heroine whose opposition to the King of Spain ended in her public execution.

Salvador Dalí was pleased that the premiere of *Mariana Pineda* would be in Barcelona and gave Lorca advice about the stage design. Federico arrived in the city to prepare for the opening.

Throughout the two-month rehearsal period, Lorca shuttled back and forth between Dalí's home in Figueras and a hotel room in Barcelona which he and Dalí sometimes shared when the painter was able to get leave from his military service duties. The curtain went up in the Goya theater the night of June 24. The actress, Margarita Xirgu, a graceful woman with a strong, square face, black eyes and a deep voice, was thirty-eight when she premiered *Mariana Pineda*. To capture Lorca's gentle heroine, she softened her usually severe makeup and concealed her dark hair under a mass of shiny blond curls. The play was well accepted and both Lorca and Xirgu appeared on the stage for the standing ovation. After so many years of frustration, the play was at last successful and was performed six times. Margarita Xirgu was delighted with the result and promised to present it in October in Madrid. Lorca clipped an article about it from a prominent newspaper and sent it to his parents with a note boasting that the news had appeared in the most important daily in Barcelona. They were impressed that their son had distinguished himself as one of the best new Andalusian poets.

Lorca sent a telegram to Dalí to tell him that the play had been well received and that his sets had been widely acclaimed. Since the two friends separated that summer, Salvador continued to work on his paintings while complaining that Margarita Xirgu had not paid him for his sets in the play. At that time, Dalí still wanted to move to Paris to join Buñuel and other Spanish artists living in the French capital.

After the premiere of *Pineda*, Lorca exhibited a series of his drawings in a café in Barcelona revealing the poet's friendship with Salvador Dalí. One of the works in Indian ink and gouache, *The Kiss*, shows Lorca's and Dalí's faces meeting in a kiss. His Barcelona drawings revealed the degree to which he had absorbed the painter's cubist aesthetic style and shared Dalí's enthusiasm for realism. After the closing of the exhibition the poet went with Salvador to

Cadaqués where he spent the remainder of July. Ana María Dalí took several photographs of Lorca in which he appeared to be very happy. At the beach, he swam only in shallow water clinging to Ana María's hand. He was terrified of drowning. Lorca felt compelled to return to Granada where his parents were becoming upset that he had been away for almost three months.

That fall, Margarita Xirgu was getting ready to present *Mariana Pineda* in Madrid on the opening night on October 12. It was a great success, with bursts of applause by the public throughout the performance delighting Federico who thought that he had made a successful debut in the theater. He was now being regarded as one of the finest poets of his generation and was also going to make a name for himself with his plays although commercially this one was a failure. It ran for only twenty-six performances, well short of the hundred that typically signaled a success.

Around that time, Lorca and the composer Manuel de Falla worked on a musical production of a play for children that he adapted from an Andalusian story. Federico designed the settings and a miniature stage and served as puppeteer engaging in impromptu dialogue with his young audience. Extremely prolific, he also finished *Suites,* a book of poems and ballads that would not be published until 1983, forty-seven years after his death.

In the fall of 1924 having returned to Madrid, Lorca read his ballads to a group of friends who crowded into the Residence to welcome him back to the capital. Among the listeners was poet and painter Rafael Alberti who thought that Lorca looked like a peasant from the south. That evening Lorca and Alberti dined together and Federico launched into an impromptu recital of his new poems. At one point, Lorca impulsively asked him to create a painting with a likeness of the Virgin beside a stream and a legend of apparition of Our Lady of Beautiful Love to the poet Federico García Lorca. A few days later Alberti returned to the Residence with the painting Lorca had requested and said that he felt like his younger brother and that they should stay in touch with each other by letter.

Dalí was back at the Residence that year and he and other friends spent hours in movie director Buñuel's room listening to jazz while sipping rum grog, a drink strictly against house rules. Late in the afternoon they often went to Lorca's room for tea, talk and smoke. The evenings typically lasted until midnight and culminated in readings from a book. Federico and Dalí wandered through Madrid together gazing at paintings in the Prado Museum and listening to jazz in local cafés. These were happy days for Lorca, full of fascinating conversation and comradeship.

In January Salvador Dalí held a very successful exhibition of his paintings. The theme of four of the twenty-three pictures shown involved Lorca. In the works *Composition with Three Figures, Table by the Sea* and *Harlequin* the head of the poet appears. These Lorca-inspired paintings show that if Federico was obsessed with Dalí, Salvador was not indifferent to the poet. After the exhibition, Dalí was recognized as a force in modern Catalan painting.

Back in Granada Federico became absorbed in preparing a literary review with a group of friends. The magazine was to appear as a supplement of the local newspaper. He requested a drawing of a rooster from Dalí, to embellish the publication, that the painter supplied.

Also, at that time Federico wrote *Poem of Cante Jondo* (Poem of Deep Song), a book that would be published in 1931. Lorca expresses his profound knowledge of flamenco. He recognized *cante jondo* was a cry of anguish emanating from profound emotions of solitude and suffering. The origin of this type of song can be traced to Arab melodies, some say, or to echoes of Jewish canticles in their synagogues. It speaks of telluric sadness emerging from the wildest of solitudes.

His work *Songs* published in May, avoids the confessional tone and romantic clichés of earlier work. With it, he achieves a new level of poetic sophistication in which he neither hides nor confesses anything although he hints at his ambivalent feelings toward love and sex, insinuating his unease with the female gender. *Songs* is a leap forward in the evolution of his style. His metaphors are sharper now. As in all of Lorca's work, there is an undertow of loss and sorrow and an acute awareness of human mortality. Awash with traditional Andalusian settings and motifs, the work shows how completely Lorca had absorbed the lore of his region.

CHAPTER 6
GYPSY BALLADS – 1928

I n December, Lorca was in the Residence to give a talk
on classic poet Luis de Góngora which turned out to be
a success. It was delivered before his departure for Seville
where he was invited by the Arts Club to participate in a
series of lectures also in honor of Góngora. The bullfighter
Ignacio Sánchez Mejías happened to be on the train from
Madrid. Lorca admired the famous matador thinking of
him as one who fulfills the metaphor of making life a duel.

The evening at the Arts Club ended up with a reading
by Lorca and Rafael Alberti of a passage from Góngora's
poem *First Solitude* (published in 1613) that generated much
enthusiasm among the audience. Afterwards Federico re-
cited some of his *Gypsy Ballads* to the delight of the public.
His audience, enthralled, stood to applaud when he fin-
ished and waved their handkerchiefs in the air as is done at
bullfights when a matador gives an exquisite performance.

At that time, Ignacio Sánchez Mejías organized a gather-
ing on his property near Seville where he invited the writers

on the condition that they dress as Arabs. Lorca, a man of many talents, entertained the party with an improvised performance of mime.

Federico returned to Granada in time for Christmas where he could again savor its unique beauty. The wintry town made him feel at peace with himself. The poet had now almost finished *The Shoemaker's Prodigious Wife* and was active on the publication, *The Cockerel*, that was to appear imminently in Granada. The magazine emphasized the death of romanticism, endorsed contemporary trends and scorned those who failed to appreciate the arts. The first issue contained Lorca's *History of this Cockerel*, an ironic description of the Grenadian temperament, several other articles by other young writers, and drawings by Salvador Dalí.

The second issue of the magazine appeared in May with the first translation into Spanish of Dali's *Manifesto Against Art* directed against the intellectual and artistic establishment and in favor of flaunting tradition. The *Manifesto* rejected all imitation of earlier art insisting on a new age free of sentimentalism. The authors listed the artists they approved of, including Lorca. After *Cockerel's* appearance for the second time, Federico returned to Madrid with his own work in mind, especially the publication of *Gypsy Ballads*.

Lorca soon became involved with Emilio Aladrén, a slender young sculptor from the School of Fine Arts, very handsome and of passionate temperament. He was constantly in trouble at the School where the leaders disapproved of his bad behavior and lack of discipline. Federico enjoyed showing him off at parties causing jealousy among his other friends, mainly his longtime partner García Carrillo. Now, Aladrén was Federico's great love and a source of joy. The two men became inseparable companions meeting nearly every night that spring in Aladren's studio where they listened to music and drank gin. Friends tried to steer Lorca away from the artist but Federico had been so utterly seduced by Emilio's youth and beauty that he allowed the sculptor to use him shamelessly.

On June 5, 1928, the poet turned thirty. His childhood was over and his adulthood loomed with its surfeit of troubles and grief. His dreams of a sweet tranquil life had evaporated. He still remained financially dependent on his parents and emotionally reliant on men like Aladrén, whose careless behavior and talk exposed Lorca to salacious gossip.

By the summer, everyone was waiting the publication of *Gypsy Ballads* which went on sale in July. To Lorca's bewilderment, it was an immediate success. At the center of the book are three poems dedicated to the cities of Granada, Córdoba and Seville, each personified as an archangel whose masculine beauty is ethereal and erotic. Seville's Saint Gabriel is described as a beautiful reed of a child; Granada's Saint Michael is a pretty boy fragrant with cologne, and Córdoba's Saint Rafael as a nude Roman on the shores of the Guadalquivir river. As sales of the book soared and the work was extolled, Federico trumpeted the news of his success to his parents and described the sudden and overwhelming frenzy of banquets, accolades and press reports. At the beginning of August, Lorca was back in Granada where his book of poetry was the most successful of all publications of the new poets. Lorca, however, was in the depths of despair; perhaps from the confusion that often follows sudden fame.

In September, Federico received a letter from Salvador Dalí in which he wrote of his dissatisfaction with *Gypsy Ballads* finding it too traditional and too tied to the lyrical norms of the past. Dalí thought that in the work, Federico showed himself as an erotic creature with his desires and his terror of death. According to him, Lorca was now a full-blown surrealist. However, Lorca's intention was to present the complicated and profound humanity of the Gypsies, a race that is proud and persecuted, courageous and feminine, artistic and dreamy, rootless but very Andalusian. *Gypsy Ballads* offers a dramatic world in which they act driven by love and hate, passion and remembrance, joy and sorrow. Their world centers on premonition and curse, on superstition and fear, a world that believes in the mortal curse of the moon and in the fatalism of passion. Thirteen of the eighteen romances in the book end in pain, disillusion or death.

The following month, the poet delivered two lectures at the Athenaeum Club in Granada. In the first he explained that for a modern poet, imagination was no longer sufficient, inspiration was. Modern poets, he said, are in search of a new reality which they approach by way of dreams. The second lecture analyzed modern painting and saw cubism and surrealism as liberating forces, freeing art from its shackles expressing the inexpressible. It was clear that Lorca saw his art as being free to express the depths of the unconscious.

Federico finished the first two parts of *Ode to the Holy Sacrament* which he had been working on since the beginning of the year. He felt this work was difficult but he hoped that his faith would help him finish it, that faith in Christ, the loving crucified Jesus friend of sinners, the lame and the sexually tormented. The poem stated that in a dehumanized, cruel world only the Jesus present in the Host offers hope. In the final part of the poem, the poet seems to write about the dignification of sexuality and suggests a rebirth of his faith. Pious Manuel de Falla, to whom the poem was dedicated, told Federico that he placed his hopes in the work.

Back in Madrid, Lorca settled into a boarding-house with his brother Francisco who was in the midst of studying for his diplomatic exams. After his three-month stay in Granada, he was content to be back in the capital and eager to see his friends. On the evening of December 13, Lorca gave a lecture on traditional Spanish lullabies at the Residence in which he described the melancholy of the laments of the peasant women who sang the Spanish folk songs he had listened to in his childhood. His address mentioned Dalí. Speaking of a bogeyman in the lullabies, Federico recalled an episode that had occurred when he visited a cubist exhibition of his friend in which a child refused to leave the gallery over some colorful pictures representing bogeymen. Lorca habitually emphasized his close friendship with the painter,

By the end of 1928, the poet declared that he was now returning to inspiration and that he found logical poetry insufferable. Instinct and passion were currently his aesthetics with a trend to the irrational rather than a search for formal perfection.

CHAPTER 7
THE LOVE OF
DON PERLIMPLÍN – 1929

Lorca, Dalí and Luis Buñuel appeared together in January in the magazine *La Gaceta Literaria*. The poet published *The Beheading of the Innocents* illustrated with drawings by Dalí showing severed heads and limbs. Buñuel presented a poem and prose text of surrealist inspiration. This was the last time the three artists were to be together in a publication. Buñuel's relationship with Dalí grew closer while he continued his attacks on Lorca, perhaps to undermine Dalí's affection for the poet. Luis had spent some time in Figueras working on the script of a film that would be called *An Andalusian Dog*. The theme contained a series of subconscious states that could be expressed only in the cinema. It is credible that the Andalusian dog of the film's title represented Lorca but Buñuel denied that it was an allusion to him. Nevertheless, the heterosexual impotence of the protagonist of the film seems to point to the poet who, according to Buñuel, was in fact impotent. Lorca was flabbergasted by the betrayal of his two old friends. In Madrid, Federico struggled to overcome his growing depression and found it difficult to muster energy to work. Besides Dali's apparent betrayal his company of the past year, Emilio Aladrén, became involved with a woman. Despite efforts to maintain a friendship he and Lorca drifted apart.

Meanwhile, a small company called The Snail was created to provide Madrid with a venue for selected theatrical plays, lectures and chamber music. Among the company's first successes was the production of Cocteau's *Orphée* and Rivas Cherif's *A Sleep of Reason*. Lorca's erotic play *The Love of Don Perlimplín* began rehearsing under the supervision of the poet but, because of its sexually suggestive content, its release was prohibited, a factor that caused Federico to sink deeper into depression.

In the spring of 1929, with his belief in himself shaken by the events of the preceding year, Federico sought a more formal return to Catholicism. Lorca's rupture with Buñuel, Dalí and Aladrén had revived his desire for spiritual purity, and he turned to the Church in search of both discipline and salvation. He continued working on his *Ode to the Most Holy Sacrament of the Altar* to be published in *Revista de Occidente*, dedicated to Manuel de Falla, hoping to honor his old friend by linking the composer's name to a poem viewed as a solemn exaltation of the Eucharist. The *Ode* is both an idiosyncratic interpretation of traditional Catholic theology and a deeply felt tribute to the qualities Christ embodies: purity, compassion, and self-sacrifice.

Lorca travelled briefly to Bilbao to deliver a lecture on Dalí and to give a poetry recital and returned to Granada on April 29 to be present at the opening of *Mariana Pineda* by Margarita Xirgu's company at the Cervantes Theater. The play was a great success with a packed house and the enthusiastic audience insisting that Federico take a bow at the end of the performance.

On May 5 a banquet in honor of the poet and Xirgu was held at the Alhambra Palace Hotel. Manuel de Falla and Fernando de los Ríos attended the festivity and so did the poet's father Don Federico Garcia. Lorca was introduced as the most brilliant of Spain's young poets. Federico responded that half his fame belonged to his native Granada that had fashioned him the way he was. Two weeks later, again at the Alhambra Palace Hotel, the poet gave a reading with excerpts from his *Book of Poems* and *Gypsy Ballads*.

A trip to New York was now underway. He received his passport on June 5 and was to depart from Southampton in England on June 19. The poet was excited and felt that it was vital for him to get away from Spain. Federico had never travelled abroad before. He was to be accompanied by Fernando de los Ríos and his niece Rita who was going to England to teach Spanish during the summer to some children in Herefordshire. On June 7, Lorca's friends in Granada gave him a send-off dinner before he left for Madrid. At Estación del Norte another group of friends gathered to bid him farewell as he boarded a train to Paris. On the train was a young American student who had first met Lorca at the Residence the previous year. Philip Cummings insisted that Lorca visit him in a wood cabin in Vermont.

The following morning the travelers arrived in Paris where Cummings left them. The crossing from Calais to

Dover was on the night of June 14 and the group spent two nights in London where they went to the British Museum and the Zoo. De los Ríos decided to visit Oxford briefly and on June 19, the two Spaniards sailed in the liner Olympic from Southampton to New York. Life was taking him in a new direction, into the cold gray swells of the Atlantic, to America.

PART 3

America

Es preciso cruzar los puentes
y llegar al rumor negro
para que el perfume de pulmón
nos golpee las sienes con su vestido
de caliente piña.

It's necessary to cross the bridges
and reach the murmuring blacks
so the perfume of their lungs
can hit our temples with its dress
of warm pineapple.

CHAPTER 8
POET IN NEW YORK – 1930

During the six-day crossing of the Atlantic Federico felt depressed and homesick wondering why he had left Spain, although in a letter to his parents, the poet assured them that he was in great shape. During the trip he befriended a five-year-old Hungarian boy who was crossing the ocean to be with his father for the first time in his life. When the two parted at the end of the journey, they both cried.

The Olympic steamed upriver, past the gray towers of Wall Street, along the docks and warehouses and apartment buildings. It was the vision that Lorca had of New York that was portrayed in the movies of the time: the tops of the skyscrapers seeming to touch the heavens, a dehumanized society controlled by robots where jazz, prohibition and organized crime prevailed. Geometry and anguish. Fernando de los Ríos must have told the poet what he might expect to find in the city. He was to stay at Columbia University, near Harlem, where he would know for the first time the problems of the Black population.

Lorca was reassured knowing that there would be two Spaniards waiting for him in the big city: Federico de Onís and Angel del Río. The sixty-three-year-old Onís had participated in the early days of the Residence in Madrid and was now the Chair of Spanish at Columbia. A distinguished philologist, he was one of the leading lights of the Spanish cultural scene in New York. Professor Angel del Río at the same university had been following Lorca's career closely and now helped mitigate his homesickness by introducing him to his friends to make him welcome.

Both Onís and del Río were at the harbor when the Olympic moored in New York. Onís arranged for Lorca's accommodation helping him to enroll as a student of English at Columbia. Once he was settled into his room, the poet wrote a letter to his parents saying that he liked the university and told them about the view from his room on the ninth floor. He described the people in the large city as naïve but charming and was impressed by the tall skyscrapers resplendent with neon advertising. He thought that New York must be the most modern city in the world. Lorca relied on his Spanish friends to shepherd him through the city. Two days after his arrival he visited Times Square at night where the sight of so many flashing lights astounded him. In August, Fernando de los Ríos left New York and Federico found himself alone except for his new circle of Spanish friends at Columbia.

At the university he pretended to enjoy his studies but he acquired almost no English during his stay in America. He learned how to order ham and eggs in a restaurant, and because it was the only dish he knew how to order, he ate ham and eggs much of the time. In English class, he spent most of the time mimicking his teacher's gestures and accent. He seemed to be afraid of English and communicated with elevator attendants with deep bows and pirouettes. His true classroom was New York. He visited the aquarium and zoo and made visits to dime stores, where he sat on the floor playing with toy horses. One evening by coincidence Lorca met a young man he had known some years back in Spain. His name was Campbell who was renting an apartment on 70th street, a classy upper east side neighborhood in Manhattan that Federico saw as an enclave where people fought each other to make money.

Meanwhile Philip Cummings, who had rented a cabin on the shores of Lake Eden, in Vermont, invited Lorca sending him the railway fare for the trip. Federico responded that he was working on his English course and that first he should finish it. He was attending class regularly as he had realized that knowing English would be useful to his career. However, he didn't make much progress and his pronunciation of the language was poor. He became a member of the Spanish House that had a library and a piano and soon was a place for Lorca's activities in New York where he spoke Spanish, played, sang folk songs, and browsed among the books in an atmosphere like the Student Residence in Madrid. He also regularly visited the Hispano-American Alliance Center where the journal of the association published English versions of Lorca's *Ballads*. Federico de Onís asked the poet to take charge of the students' choir that was to perform an evening of Spanish songs. He took this work seriously and eagerly trained the students. The concert took place in August with Federico conducting and playing the piano to the delight of everyone. His musical know-how was the main key to his success in New York. At parties, people would gather around the piano to listen Lorca play and sing Spanish songs.

Federico soon adapted to the fast pace of New York and was living this time intensely. He attended a service at a Protestant church and was surprised to see an organ in the middle of it rather than an altar. He missed the traditional dignity of Spanish Catholicism with its fervent cult to the Virgin. Contrarily, he found the service at a synagogue for Sephardic Jews moving although he missed the presence of Christ.

Lorca also met Nella Larsen, a Black author who had just published her second novel. She took Federico under her wing and together they visited Harlem where he was startled at Negroes who amused white people for profit in dance cafés, and those who celebrated the Catholic mass in church. Larsen had a party at her house with Federico being the only white person. He played the piano and sang in Spanish to the delight of the Black crowd. A young woman danced beautifully accompanied by drumming. Enchanted, the poet described the scene as the moon rising over the sea. He compared Black music to the *cante jondo* of Andalusia.

Federico began to write and in August he had finished *The King of Harlem,* a poem suggesting that Federico saw a connection between the predicament of the Blacks condemned to third-class citizenship, and the Gypsies of Andalusia who were harassed by an intolerant society. The work is a ferocious attack on the materialistic values of a capitalistic society and a plea on behalf of the Blacks. Perhaps he was foreseeing the future liberation of the Negroes and that of all oppressed minorities: Gypsies, Blacks, Jews and homosexuals. The poem *1910 (Interlude)* written by Lorca speaks of the dehumanization of the industrial society and the loneliness of modern man cut off from nature.

Escaping the heat of summer in the city, on August 16 Federico boarded a train for Vermont where Philip Cummings and his father were at the station of Montpelier to meet him. After the hustle and bustle and the concrete of New York, the poet was pleased to find himself in the lush countryside. Nonetheless, the initial good feeling turned to depression after ten days of living in a rainy climate and dark dense woods. He found the landscape beautiful but sad and managed to write three poems during his stay in the small town of Eden: *Double Poem of Lake Eden, Live Sky* and *Earth and Moon* that revealed his state of mind as he lamented being cheated by a society that robbed him of his sense of worth. Finally, he took a train back to New York on August 29.

In a more pleasant stay, the poet spent three weeks with Angel del Río and his wife Amelia in their rented cabin at Bushnellsville, New York, happy to be among Spanish friends although his depression had not lifted. However, he was able to relax, take walks, sing songs study English with Amelia. He befriended the two children of the farm's caretaker and months after leaving Bushnellsville he composed a poem about the two children portraying them as emblems of innocence in a menacing world.

Lorca had been away from Manhattan for just over one month when he returned to the busy city on September 21 and settled into a cell-like cubicle on the twelfth floor of a building at Columbia University. It was a small place but the view from its window was magnificent. To the north he could see the dark curve of the Hudson River and the George Washington bridge, then under construction. He made friends with two Spanish-speaking American students who lived a few doors down the hall. He dropped in at all hours of the day and night to talk about art, American Blacks or the Gypsies and Arabs in Spain. He liked to dramatize the most insignificant events of his daily life, and he revealed his persistent curiosity about death.

Through friends he met several of New York's most ardent hispanophiles. Among them was a soft-spoken southerner named Herschel Brickell, an executive at the publishing house Henry Holt & Company. Brickell and his wife Norma lived in a lavish apartment on Park Avenue; their living room held a new concert grand piano that Federico played regularly enthralling other guests with his renditions of Spanish folk songs. Herschel was mesmerized by Lorca's lively and eloquent wit which seemed to flutter as quickly as his hands, however, he was struck by his mood swings. One moment he was a capricious child and then suddenly he turned into an ageless creature plumbing to the depths of evil as often as he soared to the heights of good. It was this darker side of himself that Lorca continued to voice in his poetry.

Federico de Onís took Lorca to his country house at Newburgh where they arrived on September 18 and stayed before returning to Columbia University where the poet is invited to visit Havana in early 1930. The poet's last months in New York were ones of intense literary activity, writing *Childhood and Death* which reflects the poet's negative state of mind about his sexual misery, perhaps remembering his school years when the other children called him Federica.

In his new lodging at Columbia, Federico befriended a young student, John Crow, who lived on the same floor. Crow often accompanied him on his walks in the city and to jazz clubs in Harlem. Crow sensed that Lorca was tormented and lonely in spite of the fact that he was behaving like any other masculine man. Another Spaniard, José Antonio Rubio, arrived in New York at the end of October to study economics at Columbia. Rubio was aware of the poet's homosexuality and of his relationship in Spain with Emilio Aladrén.

Perhaps Lorca's most dramatic experience in the city was when the stock market crashed. For several hours he joined the crowd outside the New York Stock Exchange building, in lower Manhattan, watching people shrieking, fainting, and even committing suicide. He was very affected by what was happening and his anti-capitalism views strengthened even more. The spectacle of Black Tuesday confirmed his perception of the United States as a spiritless nation controlled by a few bankers. Shocked by the economic crisis and the confusion it spawned, he began to write a new series of poems. By the end of 1929 he had completed at least five of them.

Eventually, what Lorca thought would be two books of American poems became a single collection entitled *Poet in New York* that would be published posthumously in 1940. In the collection's best poems facts blend with fiction, and language with emotion, to yield both a public indictment of urban society and a private cry of despair. It is an example of Lorca's stage as a super realist, a reaction against the abstract intellectualism of cubist writers. The work postulates a fantastic environment without ties to reality in which the poet explores the world of the subconscious, dealing with what is human and at the same time infrahuman. In New York, the human suffering he witnessed moved him closer to a Marxist perception of the human condition.

At the end of October, Lorca wrote to his parents about some rich American friends wanting to sponsor the production of *Don Perlimplín*. One of these friends may have been María Antonieta Rivas who said the poet could be better known as a playwright. Lorca also commented about the new theater existing in New York producing modern plays and Black musicals that he found to be beautiful and sensitive. Federico also saw some Chinese theater with its traditional lack of scenery but with a special skill for mime. All of these theatrical experiences impressed Lorca and probably influenced his development as a playwright.

In December, Lorca joined the Brickells on Christmas Eve at their home where they had set up a small shrine for the Virgin with a candle for each of their guests to light while they made a wish. Federico was touched and was glad to read passages from his *Don Perlimplín*. At midnight, he was taken to midnight mass at the Catholic church of Saint Paul the Apostle and couldn't help being nostalgic for Christmas Eve in Granada with his family. In February 1930, he wrote the poem *Christmas* in which he depicted the bitter solitude of man destined to live in a materialistic society.

Lorca was now an addict of the new 'talkies' and felt that he could try his hand at films with sound in which you could hear the sighs, the breeze, the noises perfectly reproduced. He knew of the rave reviews of Buñuel's *Un Chien Andalou* and, no doubt, felt the urge to emulate this work. In fact, he worked on a script of a film trying to describe parts of New York life as he saw it. Lorca's surrealist film-script *Trip to the Moon* was about a physical journey towards the moon symbolic of death, in search of a love that proves impossible. The connection to Buñuel's film is evident, using erotic imagery including a close-up of female genitalia and the sense of mutilated sexuality. *Trip to the Moon* can be seen as Lorca's own progress towards sexual annihilation. In the film, the character Elena is highlighted in a context of violence and horror. It is possible that Lorca knew of the relationship between Dalí and Gala whose real name was Helena of whom the poet may have been jealous. Or perhaps it was a reference to Eleonor Dove, Emilio Aladrén's English fiancée. *Trip to the Moon* never made it to the screen.

Federico continued showing concern for the Jewish citizens of New York and for the Blacks who in his mind were the true artists in the United States. He sees the metropolis as a gigantic machine that negates nature and promotes artificiality. The subjects of his poems included Wall Street, Harlem, the Brooklyn Bridge and the small Jewish Cemetery. He wrote the *Landscape of the Vomiting Multitude*, a poem about Coney Island crowds at sunset, describing the effect of alcoholic drinks sold in those prohibition days to people not able to afford to deal with reliable bootleggers whose drinks were easier to digest. It was a work stinking of death, disgust, horror and pity set in landscapes of cemeteries, hospitals and wharfs where drunken sailors reeled under the moon.

In the middle of January, guitar-player Andrés Segovia arrived in New York to give a series of recitals. Segovia and Lorca attended several parties together, and on January 21 Federico gave his first lecture in America on lullabies. On

February 10 the Instituto de las Españas honored Lorca prior to a departure he had scheduled for Cuba, with the poet giving a lecture on surrealism in theory and practice. On February 6, Ignacio Sánchez Mejías and his artist fiancée arrived in New York. Lorca attended her concerts and worked with her on the harmonization of Spanish popular songs which they would record when back in Spain, and Ignacio gave a lecture on bullfighting.

On March 4, Lorca took a train for Tampa where he embarked on the American steamer Cuba, which arrived the following afternoon in Havana. In New York, a newspaper commented that the poet had left Manhattan more Spanish, more Andalusian and more Grenadian than ever. In fact, in his dislike of the metropolis and in a hostile environment, the poet had come to appreciate how much he loved his native Spain. On the other hand, New York had given him what he later described as the most useful experience of his life. He left the United States with renewed faith in his work, a more compassionate understanding of his sexuality, and a newfound enthusiasm for life.

Meanwhile, the situation in Spain changed dramatically with the fall on January 28 of the dictator Primo de Rivera and his replacement by General Dámaso Berenguer who promised general elections. Fernando de los Ríos expressed his conviction that a new Spain was about to be born.

CHAPTER 9
CUBA – 1930

Lorca's earliest impressions of Cuba were from the labels of the cigars his father received from the island and from the habaneras (songs of Havana) sung by his Aunt Isabel. Nearly everything reminded him of home. In downtown Havana he could hear people singing the same slow, sad songs he knew and he could smell the aroma of coffee and magnolias. What was to have been a brief visit to Cuba quickly would become a three-month stay.

The poet José Chacón was waiting for him in Cuba, and Federico was sure that his time there was going to be exciting. For days the Havana newspapers had been announcing the arrival of Federico, so well- known for his *Gypsy Ballads*. He was seen as the most representative voice of a new generation of Spanish poets. The presence of the young Andalusian would start a debate between the upholders of modern poetry and those who wanted to maintain traditional verse. On the quayside were representatives of the Hispano-Cuban Institution which had invited him. The journalist Rafael Suárez had informed his readers of the arrival of a revolutionary Spanish poet.

Lorca stayed at the Hotel La Unión in the middle of a labyrinth of narrow streets like those in Andalusia. He thought that Havana was like a big Cádiz where people spoke very loudly. Andalusia and Cuba seemed to be linked by temperament and culture, and Cuba's music influenced by that of Spain. Soon, the poet went native for Cuban culture regarding the island as a paradise. He loved its orchids, the sugarcane stalks, the tropical fruits and the exotic names of its desserts. He sought opportunities to meet ordinary Cuban people: fishermen, busboys and poverty-stricken villagers struggling to survive. Lorca was impressed by the young mulattos with their astonishing athletic bodies.

Federico met Antonio Quevedo who with his wife María Muñoz founded the Bach Music Conservatory. Manuel de Falla had sent a letter to them introducing the poet and asking them to take good care of him. Cuba received him with open arms. Lorca gave five lectures that were very successful, well attended and given ample coverage by the Havana newspapers. The poet wrote to his parents about the generous hospitality he was receiving and his joy at the success of his lectures.

Federico made friends with the Loynaz family, four brothers and sisters famous for their wealth and eccentricity who lived in splendor in a mansion surrounded by a tropical garden with porcelain, sculptures, French furniture, pictures and other treasures. Lorca loved the house, especially the white peacocks and flamingoes in the garden. He made the house his base in Havana and never returned to his hotel before dawn. Federico read to the family scenes from *Yerma* a play whose origin reached back to the poet's childhood when pilgrimages were made to the nearby village of Moclín where Christ of the Cloth is said to have cured cases of impotence and infecundity. When a child in Fuente Vaqueros, Federico must have seen people passing through the Vega on their way to the hermitage. At the same time, Lorca was also working on *Doña Rosita the Spinster* which the poet sang at the piano.

Federico befriended Fernando Ortiz, an expert in Afro-Cuban culture who informed him of the many rites of African origin on the island. His sister-in-law, Lidia Cabrera, invited the poet to a secret ceremony known for its magic and the occult. Lorca's obsession with death might have gotten him interested in the performance. He also met the Guatemalan poet Luis Cardoza who was the consul of that country in Havana. Together, they visited the Teatro Alhambra that specialized in satire of the corruption that prevailed on the island at the time. The theater was a men-only venue where pornographic plays were also performed. Federico was delighted to attend the shows and proposed to his friend to write a farce together of grotesque and blasphemous content.

Cardoza didn't recount any homosexual amorous activity of Lorca in Cuba. Although rumors were circulating in Havana where gossip was rampant, no episode in particular could be verified. However, it seems true that the poet had a relationship with a mulatto called Lamadrid. In Cuba, he learned not only to accept his homosexuality but to rejoice in it.

Meanwhile, Lorca continued writing *The Public*, a play that he seems to have conceived in New York and nearly finished in Cuba before his return to Spain. The work was a dramatic play that explored the theme of homosexual love. In it, Lorca makes an impassioned plea for the right of the individual to love according to his needs. The work was a play within a play, which follows Shakespeare's *A Midsummer Night's Dream* that the poet admired, finding it a vindication of all expressions of love, including homosexual. Throughout the play, the protagonist denounces the duplicity that prevents people from being themselves to live their sexuality. *The Public* seems to reflect the anguish that took hold of Federico when his relationships with Aladrén ended. In fact, the work was angry and bitter about the suffering of a writer condemned by an unjust society to mask his true self.

The historian Emilio Roig, a frequent contributor to a local magazine who admired Lorca's work, decided not to meet the poet alleging that he didn't participate in the struggle against Spanish dictator Primo de Rivera's persecution of intellectuals and that he was, in fact, apolitical. However, Roig discovered afterwards that Federico was very much concerned about injustice, both in Cuba and in Spain. The truth is that the poet was opposed to all dictatorships and that he even was a supporter of the Cuban opposition politicians.

On May 16, one of Lorca's best friends, the musicologist Adolfo Salazar, arrived in Havana to give a series of lectures. As a homosexual himself, Salazar knew more about Federico than many of his close friends. He found the poet to be more Andalusian than ever but at the same time the Gypsy rhythms of his blood had fused with the blood of the Blacks in Cuba. His *cante jondo* was soothed in the swaying cadence of the Afro-Cuban *son* (sound), a sinuous rumba-like dance accompanied by marimbas, bongo drums and maracas. The *son* inspired the only poem Lorca is known to have written in Cuba, *Blacks Dancing to Cuban Rhythms*. Fusing childhood impressions and contemporary images of the island, he produced a songlike poem in which figures from his father's cigar boxes combine with tobacco plants, crocodiles, palm trees, and rum to create a moving tribute to a country Lorca had come to love. He published the work that spring in the Cuban journal *Musicalia*.

Lorca, Salazar and Cardoza were about to leave Cuba when a lunch was held at the Hotel Bristol in their honor. There were speeches about the sadness at the departure of the three writers whose presence in Havana had been so wonderfully impactful. Flor Loynaz, of the household where he had spent much of his time, helped the poet pack his belongings and drove him to the harbor in her Fiat, arriving in time to embark on the Manuel Arnus liner. Lorca assured everyone present that he had spent the happiest days of his life on the island.

On June 18, the transatlantic docked in New York but Federico couldn't go ashore because his visa had expired. Lorca sent a telegram to Federico de Onís and other friends asking them to visit him on board. He organized a party and played Andalusian songs on the piano accompanied by everyone merrily singing. The poet sang numerous Spanish and Cuban rhythms during the crossing of the Atlantic with passengers and crew joining in.

At sea, Lorca resumed work on his *Ode to Walt Whitman*. The work would stand as a testament to the emotional and sexual metamorphosis he had undergone in America.

PART 4

The Republic

Bañó con sangre enemiga
su corbata carmesí,
pero eran cuatro puñales
y tuvo que sucumbir.

Covered with the enemy's blood
his scarlet tie,
but there were four daggers
and he had to go down.

CHAPTER 10
THE SHOEMAKER'S PRODIGIOUS LIFE – 1930

When the liner docked at Cádiz, Federico was met by his brother Francisco and sister Isabel who had driven from Granada to greet him. The reunion was an emotional occasion. The press in Granada announced his arrival and described the poet's achievements in America where he spread the prestige of Spanish literature. Interviewed, he mentioned New York's extra-human architecture and furious rhythm, geometry and anguish with man and machine both living in the slavery of the moment. He complained about the army of windows, where no single person has time to look at a cloud or to carry on a conversation. He went on to describe the Negroes as the most spiritual and delicate element in that world, because they believe, hope, sing and have an exquisite religious languor that relieves their anxieties. On the other hand, he says Wall Street is impressive because it is cold and cruel. Gold flows there in rivers from every part of the world and death comes with it. Nowhere else does one feel the total absence of the spirit. No one could have any idea of the loneliness which a Spaniard feels there, above all a man from Andalusia.

Lorca returned to Spain a more brash, more sardonic man. He settled easily back into the routines of country life at the Huerta de San Vicente. He padded around the house in his pajamas, content to play the piano while the rest of the family went about their business. His sister Concha, married to his friend Manuel Fernández-Montesinos, was expecting her first child and his mother was jubilant at having Federico back near her.

During the summer of 1930 the political situation in Spain was a constant topic of discussion in the poet's home. The dictator Miguel Primo de Rivera had died in exile and there was uncertainty about the monarchy as King Alfonso XIII was losing the support of the people. The Republicans believed that their time had come as the new president General Dámaso Berenguer, promised national elections in the country. Meanwhile, Fernando de los Ríos was back at Granada University since the fall of Primo de Rivera advocating for the coming of democracy, and various political groups pledged to work towards the downfall of the regime.

At this time, Emilio Aladrén wrote to Federico telling him that he was delighted about his return to Spain. The two would renew their friendship that autumn in Madrid.

At the end of the summer, Lorca's family spent some weeks in coastal Málaga, one of Federico's favorite cities. There, the poet learned that Dalí and his wife Gala had been nearby in the town of Torremolinos where she was convalescing from an attack of pleurisy.

In October, Lorca travelled back to Madrid where he was interviewed about his American experience. He announced that he had three books ready for press: *Earth and Moon, Odes* and *New York,* a poetic interpretation of the American metropolis, much of it devoted to the Blacks.

One evening, Lorca read *The Public* to a group of friends who were gathered in the elegant apartment of Carlos and Bebé Lynch. When he finished, the room fell silent. Lynch claimed that the play was so disturbing that if staged, it would provoke a scandal. Federico thought that his friends had not understood the work and that if produced it would be a great success. However, when the play premiered in Madrid some fifty years afterwards, many who saw it found it baffling. In fact, the play appeared to be scarcely more than a miscellany of loosely connected images and ideas. Throughout the script Lorca repeats lines, actions, and images so that the characters echo one another in voice and appearance but, on the other hand, it is the author's fiercest challenge to the bourgeois crowds who filled Spain's theaters with their hidebound taste and polite expectations. The poet was calling for nothing less than the abolition of theater as he knew it. However, it was agreed between Federico, Rivas Cherif and Margarita Xirgu that the more acceptable, *The Shoemaker's Prodigious Wife* would be performed at the Teatro Español in Madrid.

Meanwhile, on December 12 a group of rebel republican officers staged an uprising in the town of Jaca. The conspiracy failed, the insurrection was crushed and the two military officers responsible were shot. Three days later, it was the Madrid rebels' turn to start an uprising, but the insurrection was quickly put down by the police. Several left-wing party members and politicians were arrested, including Fernando de los Ríos and the future president of the republic Alcalá Zamora. Nevertheless, although the insurrection had failed, it was clear that the monarchy would soon fall. From jail, De los Ríos and his colleagues in the republican movement continued to agitate for a new government, issuing a manifesto to the people of Spain demanding a republic based on national sovereignty and represented by a constituent assembly. Lorca himself kept aloof from politics.

A few weeks later, on December 24, Lorca's work *The Shoemaker's Prodigious Wife* was staged at Teatro Español. The play was a farce conceived by the author as a ballet without music. In an Andalusian village, a young woman marries an old shoemaker who was fifty-three years old. They don't have children and quarrel often. She is a pretty girl who dreams of travelling to faraway places rather than taking care of the household chores. A despairing husband flees home for a while and returns some time afterwards disguised as a teller of crimes and miracles. The young wife likes him but when he comes back as the shoemaker, she rejects him again. Lorca's joyful, dynamic play is an example of his literary genius. The opening was a success, and the public loved the superb acting of Margarita Xirgu. The show ran for thirty additional performances encouraging the poet to continue writing for the theater. Nevertheless, over the next few years Federico would try in vain to have *The Public* produced and in view of the failure he turned to his Andalusian themes that he knew so well.

After spending Christmas and the New Year with his family in Granada, Federico returned to Madrid in January of

1931 where the theater world was finding a stiff competition from the film industry. The political situation was shaky after the government of General Berenguer, prime minister of King Alfonso XIII, resigned in mid-February. A new cabinet was formed by Juan Bautista Aznar, also from the monarchy, who promised municipal, not general, elections in April. Meanwhile, Lorca had been busy releasing a series of records of Spanish folk songs harmonized by the poet. Critics in Spain as well as and South America were enthusiastic.

At the time, Federico and his brother Francisco were living in an apartment in Madrid. Francisco was preparing his exam to enter the diplomatic corps. The morning of April 11, French poet Matilde Pomés went to the flat to hear Lorca play songs he had learned in Cuba on the piano. Pomés had known the poet in Paris in 1929 and was excited to meet him again in Madrid. Together, they went to the restaurant where a group of the best poets of the day were waiting. During lunch, besides literature, the group discussed the municipal elections to be held the following day. On Sunday April 12, 1931, the polls opened at eight in the morning and Spaniards flocked to the polling stations. Lorca was sitting in a café on a square which was filling rapidly with a noisy crowd shouting against the regime. The police charged the throng causing panic.

Later in the day, Lorca and friends joined a republican demonstration marching in the street towards Plaza de Cibeles which was protected by police on horseback. Shots rang and the marchers again disbanded in panic, Lorca and his friend Matilde included.

That night, the election results were known. Contrary to expectations, the Spanish monarchy won the municipal election, in large part because the country's powerful landowners ensured the victory in the countryside. But in the cities, pro-monarchy candidates lost heavily. Despite the monarchy's numerical victory, it was clear to most that Spaniards wanted a new government.

Given the sentiment for a republic and to prevent civil war, King Alfonso XIII stepped down. Two days later, the Second Spanish Republic was proclaimed. The possibility of a new democratic country was now a reality. On Tuesday, April 14, at approximately four o'clock, a republican flag rose slowly above the main post office building in the Plaza de Cibeles. People poured into the streets, chanting the Marseillaise and the International, the revolutionary workers' songs. By nightfall, the news was official: King Alfonso XIII would leave Spain.

Earlier in the day, officials had released the jailed leaders of the republican movement, among them was Lorca's friend Fernando de los Ríos, who was quickly named minister of justice in a new republican cabinet. The new leaders wasted no time in implementing their radical agenda. They changed the Spanish flag and the national anthem, as well as a number of streets names to republican-inspired ones. They scheduled elections for a constituent parliament, introduced agrarian reforms and secularized schools, hospitals and cemeteries.

One of the Republic's greatest battles was fought in the field of public education, which had been controlled until then by the Catholic Church. The government of the new Spain was determined to end this monopoly and create a system to meet the challenges posed by widespread illiteracy estimating that many new schools needed to be created, 7,000 in the first year and 5,000 over the following four years. It turned out that in two and half years, over 13,500 schools were opened. It was an amazing achievement. Together with the building of schools, the government planned to raise the status of teaching professionals, especially those who were elementary teachers. Salaries were improved by 50 percent and 5,000 new positions created. Besides schools, the Republic proposed to legalize divorce and reduce the number of religious orders. Lorca spoke out in favor of these initiatives and announced that he would volunteer as a music teacher.

The reaction of the Catholic Church was swift and hostile. On May 7, 1931, Cardinal Segura, Archbishop of Toledo, attacked the reforms in his pastoral letter, referring to the dangerous threat posed to the rights of the Church and asked the women of Spain to organize a crusade of prayers to counteract such proposals. He implied that the newly inaugurated republic was virtually communist and that by separating church and state, the republicans had infringed on the Catholic hierarchy.

Four days later, six convents and a Jesuit building were set on fire in Madrid. In the wake of the burnings, the republican government declared martial law and authorized the use of the Civil Guard to prevent further violence. The right now had grounds to attack the anti-clerical republicans by hardening Catholic opposition to the new regime.

In the five following years, the governments of the Republic would span three well-defined periods. From 1931 to 1933, the country had a strong republican government headed by Manuel Azaña. Then from November 1933 to January of 1936 power swung to a right-wing coalition in which the largest group was the Spanish Confederation of Autonomous Right-Wing Groups (CEDA), a new middle-class Catholic party; this period was referred as the Black Biennium. Despite its success in the 1933 elections, CEDA failed to achieve a total majority in parliament but insisted on suppressing the rights of the working classes in favor of privileges for the conservatives. This produced a violent reaction on the left and a series of retaliatory strikes were soon organized by the trade unions. Finally, from February 1936 to July, when the civil war broke out, Spain was run by the leftish Popular Front.

Back in Granada, Lorca continued working, having finished two new plays titled *When Five Years Pass* and *Blood Wedding* to be presented by Margarita Xirgu. Also, he completed a book of poetry, *Poems of the Dead* that he considered the most intense he had written to date. He had been working passionately day and night. In *When Five Years Pass* the poet wrote about the future, the certainty of death and the impossibility of sexual fulfilment, with numerous allusions to the protagonist's impotence.

At the end of the summer, Federico tried to get away from Granada for a visit to a friend in Santander, but his parents wanted to keep him with them. So instead, the poet went to Fuente Vaqueros where the republican town council invited him to inaugurate the public library whose creation he had recommended two years earlier. Lorca spoke about books as performing a vital role in forming free men and women very much in tune with republican desires. He argued that true wisdom lies in the contrasting of ideas and that the library should be space for both the mystics and the revolutionaries, those authors who believe in the love for humanity and the elevation of the spirit akin to their high idealism. Federico ended his speech by telling the audience that he believed in a classless society and that he approved of its evolution. For that society to become a reality, culture was vital and required sacrifice. The address left no doubt that Lorca was aligned with the Republic and that his views were strongly anti-capitalistic. Federico believed like Fernando de los Ríos that the Republic should be the beginning of a new adventure in the history of Spain.

With the help of his friend, writer Martínez Nadal, Lorca made up his mind to publish *Poem of the Deep Song* that he had begun writing in 1921. The 171-page volume came out in late May 1931, shortly before Federico's thirty-third birthday. It went on sale in June, accompanied by an advertising campaign promoting the collection as the great poet's expression in its purest, most brilliant form. Critics responded favorably, describing the work as a book of 'mystical poetry that opens the reader to the infinite.'

On May 29, 1931, the government of the Republic created an organization called Teaching Missions presided over by Manuel Bartolomé Cossío, an art historian and teacher colleague of Francisco Giner de los Ríos at the Residence. The goal of the body was to take the message of the new democratic Spain to underprivileged people in poor villages by putting on plays, performing concerts, helping local teachers, organizing art exhibitions and setting up libraries. The mission attracted the country's best writers and artists, including Lorca who was present at the new parliament to hear a speech by Fernando de los Ríos on the current religious controversy. In his opinion, the Catholic Church had been strangling the life of the country for more than five hundred years and he recalled the abuses of the Inquisition. Merged with an oppressive monarchy, the church had persecuted, burned, and expelled the Spanish Jews.

Now Spaniards had the right to live and educate their children as they pleased. What De los Ríos proclaimed was some compromise which would permit the building of a democratic society without violence. But it was not to be. Liberals demanded fast measures, while conservatives did not agree with De los Ríos' analysis of the role of the church in Spanish history. Head of CEDA José María Gil Robles responded with a speech that explained the position of conservatives regarding the church and its relationship to the Republic. It was becoming clear that compromise in Spain was going to be difficult if not impossible.

Lorca went home to Granada in July and by mid-August he finished a new book of poetry that he called *Poems of the Dead*. The work was never published but it seemed that its stark imagery and opaque language were reminiscent of his New York poems.

In August, Lorca completed a new play, *Once Five Years Pass*, which like *The Public*, he continued to read to select friends. The new drama was another attempt to shatter the bounds of mainstream theater. Lorca had conceived the play before going home to Granada that summer and had talked about it with Carlos and Bebé Lynch who expressed their enthusiasm for the work. He appears to have written the play in its entirety that summer dating the manuscript August 19, 1931. In the work, two lovers agree to wait five years before marrying but when five years have passed, the young woman abandons her fiancé for a virile soccer player. The young man in desperation pursues a second woman but she too scorns him saying that she will marry him after five years pass.

The play is both a dreamlike meditation on the phenomenon of time and a deliberate obfuscation of conventional theatrical performance. Lorca's distortion of time reflects his own fascination with the subject and that of his contemporaries, especially Salvador Dalí who in 1931 completed his painting *The Persistence of Memory*. The play is in many ways a private elegy, scattered with figures and events from Lorca's past: a child's funeral, a dead cat, a boy who used to wear a clown's costume whenever he came to play with Federico and his siblings. Lorca described the work as being a mystery play, written in prose and verse, whose theme is the passage of time.

In the late summer, republican fervor gripped the Vega. Shortly after the proclamation of the new regime in April, residents of Fuente Vaqueros called for the abolition of the death penalty. In the spirit of a new and secular Spain they had also renamed one of the village's streets Calle Federico García Lorca in honor of the town's most famous son. At the end of September Lorca returned to Madrid where the newly elected politicians had begun drafting a constitution.

On October 16, Manuel Azaña became prime minister and quickly forged a coalition with the party's socialist constituency. Lorca attended a session of the parliament where he watched as his old friend and teacher Fernando de los Ríos, now minister of justice, gave an inflammatory speech calling for the complete separation of church and state. De los Ríos assailed the Catholic Church for its stranglehold on the country's intellectual life and spoke with regret of the Jews who had been expelled from Spain in 1492. Liberals applauded the speech while conservatives blasted It. Azaña was a distinguished writer and excellent orator who soon became one of the republican politicians most hated by conservatives.

Lorca was aware of the issues at stake in the country and was determined to participate in the shaping of the New Spain by being involved in the creation of a university traveling theater, called La Barraca (The Barn), which would perform classical works in rural villages. He immediately identified himself with the project expressing his wish to become its artistic director. Participating university students were to take their performances to the villages during their vacations. On November 25, Fernando de los Ríos declared his support for La Barraca. Five days later the Spanish Students' Union formally requested government funding for the company arguing that the primary purpose of the group was to provide rural people the opportunity to see plays without having to travel to the cities. The University Theater received a government grant of 100,000 pesetas (about $700) annually for purchasing equipment, vans, the construction of a portable stage and to cover other costs.

Meanwhile, Lorca was named artistic director and with his colleagues began working hard to prepare the company's first tour. He was able to count on the help of artist friends who designed the sets. The stage measured only eight by eight yards and didn't have elaborate décor so it could be erected and dismantled quickly. The official uniform of La Barraca was a blue coverall for men and a simple blue and white dress for girls.

Conservatives soon took issue with the state-subsidized enterprise which they considered to be cover to spread marxist propaganda. In January 1932, a satirical right-wing newspaper ridiculed the troupe and its director. It mocked Lorca, calling him a Gypsy and De los Ríos a Sephardic Jew. Two weeks later, the prime minister told members of the parliament that La Barraca signaled the start of a new spiritual world in Spain, a world of collaboration between the classes, of fraternity among men.

Lorca primarily aimed to revive and exalt the great plays of the Spanish Golden Age, as the years of great Spanish artistic creativity from 1492 to 1659, are called. He adapted some short plays and 17th century Calderon de la Barca's *Life is a Dream* which some viewed as a Catholic dilemma. In fact, the reason for Lorca to include this play was that it had musical parts which he considered to be 'real theater.' Federico himself played the part of a shadow that represented death moving across the stage. He insisted on imposing his criteria in the training of the actors' movements, gestures and diction. Slowly but surely, during the first six months La Barraca developed a style unlike that of any professional company then performing in Spain. Two dozen students were selected to perform. Lorca wanted the troupe to be egalitarian so he insisted on a democratic and cordial camaraderie. No one received a salary, having joined the company for idealistic reasons. Rehearsals began in early 1932 and, as artistic director, Lorca drove his young cast relentlessly. He also paid close attention to its music frequently embellishing nonmusical texts by adding popular songs and melodies to the original script.

While preparations for the theater were going ahead, Lorca gave a series of lectures in Valladolid, Seville, Vigo, Santiago de Compostela, La Coruña, Salamanca, Madrid and San Sebastián. Federico was delighted to have returned to Galicia, particularly to Santiago with its impressive cathedral. He read *A Poet in New York* which was received with enthusiasm. A critic wrote that it was the greatest achievement in contemporary Spanish poetry.

While in Salamanca, the poet met with philosopher Miguel de Unamuno who had been reinstated as rector at the university after having been exiled by the dictator Primo de Rivera. The rector invited him and some friends to take a walk around the old city. Between March 16 and May 29, Federico delivered a total of six lectures. As speaker the great poet gave casual readings from notes scribbled on odd-sized sheets of paper.

On July 10 La Barraca departed for the town of Burgo de Osma in the province of Soria. The caravan consisted of several vehicles carrying the portable stage, the sets and the rest of the equipment and student actors. In the evening the town square was packed to listen to the introduction by Lorca. The production was a great success; the audience loved the sets and the acting of the students. The next stops were San Leonardo and Vinuesa where people were suspicious but eventually the representation went quite well. In Soria, the capital of the province, the play didn't go as expected. There were interlopers, monarchist students who had travelled from Madrid with the intention of ensuring that La Barraca's first performance in a provincial capital would be a failure. So, it was. The next stop was Almazán where this time the audience of mostly peasants enjoyed the show. The company rounded off its first tour by giving a performance in the Student Residence in Madrid.

The news of what had happened in Soria reached the capital where the right-wing press twisted the incident to discredit the group and Fernando de los Ríos and all those involved with the new University Theater, particularly Lorca, making insinuations regarding his homosexuality. According to the extreme right, Federico was now an enemy of true Spain, country of the sword and the Church. La Barraca's enemies were also against the student actresses of the University Theater, insinuating that they were promiscuous and spreading rumors of their immorality. Despite all these attacks, Lorca was satisfied with the outcome of the first tour and the favorable reaction of the spectators in the small towns. Consequently, the poet talked about plans for a second tour in late August when they hoped to perform modern European plays. There was no doubt that La Barraca was on its way to becoming one of the most exciting cultural experiments of the time.

In the summer, Lorca returned to his Huerta de San Vicente in Granada with the purpose of finishing *Blood Wedding* which he completed in a few weeks working day and night. Federico's stay in the Huerta coincided with the staging of a military coup by General José Sanjurjo against the government. The insurrection failed but it made clear that there was an ongoing right-wing conspiracy against the Republic.

CHAPTER 11
BLOOD WEDDING – 1932

I n 1932, Lorca began the first of a trilogy of rural trag-
edies written in his last years. Unlike *The Public* and *Once
Five Years Pass*, the new work, *Blood Wedding*, was a three-act
play that had strong ties to both classical and popular tra-
ditions. He had envisioned it in 1928, but it was four years
later, in the flush of his achievement with La Barraca and
his renewed exposure to the classics of the Spanish Golden
Age, that he brought himself to compose the work.

The play was inspired by an assassination that took
place in the 1920's in the Andalusian village of Níjar in the
province of Almería. In the actual event, a young woman,
Francisca, lived on a prosperous farm near Níjar with her
father. Local gallants were enticed by her good looks and
charm, along with a dowry which her father would provide
when she married. However, she became engaged to a mod-
est laborer, Casimiro, who was pressured by his brother and
sister-in-law to marry the heiress as a good opportunity to
move up in life. Francisca, for her part, was in love with a

Bodas de Sangre (written in 1932). Tragic play set in rural Spain in a society that values marriage for profit more than marriage for love.

more appealing young man, Curro Montes, who, the night before her wedding, ran away with her. He was consequently killed by the groom's cousin.

Lorca dwells on themes of love, honor and vengeance. He resents the reality that women in this environment have almost no control over their own lives and loves, he disdains that fact that marriages are made for money, and he has a horror of honor killing. In his version of the Níjar tragedy, neither bride nor bridegroom are given names. However, he gives the name Leonardo Félix, who now has a wife and child, to the bride's previous lover. His surname is important because it specifies that he belongs to a family which has a longstanding feud with the bride's kin (à la Romeo and Juliet). Shortly after her wedding, Leonardo steals the willing bride and the lovers flee on horseback.

Male family members pursue the couple through a dark forest, the personified helpful moon lighting the way, and, after furious words, the bridegroom and Leonardo slay each other.

Lorca wrote this modern tragedy in a setting that captures the flavor of life lived in rural Andalusian tradition, with its folk poetry, music and speech. Leonardo's mother tells of her family's blood spilled over time in fights with the enemy clan and prophesizes the impending tragedy. She becomes possessed by the fear of extinction of her bloodline and by an anxiety to see her physical existence perpetuated by her son's children in a social order in which women are valued only for the sons they produce.

Lorca used his knowledge of Andalusian folklore to present the lovely wedding songs of the second act, and he chose concise language true to the rural spirit of the play with a vocabulary that reflects the coarseness of local farmers. In *Blood Wedding*, the poet succeeds in creating a setting that allows him to express his deepest concerns, those of love and death.

Lorca talked on and off to friends about the themes of this story central to his work: illicit love, sacrificial death, revenge and the power of human instinct. With *Blood Wedding*, Federico sought both to reimagine the events that had taken place in Níjar and to revive classic theater. He had long viewed rural Spanish life, with its stark blend of Catholic dogma and pagan superstition, as innately tragic.

Lorca's experience with La Barraca reinforced his belief in the theater's ancient ties to the people. More than ever, he was convinced that if twentieth-century Spanish theater was to be saved it must return both to the people and to tragedy. After completing the work, he must have sensed that it could reach a mass audience. The play was to premier the following spring in Madrid's Teatro Beatriz with the actress Josefina Díaz Artigas and her company and Lorca himself as director.

Meanwhile in August La Barraca travelled to Galicia and Asturias to perform in several localities. The tour went smoothly and in most towns the routine was the same. The troupe arrived by truck and selected a performance site, often in a square backed by a church or civic building, and as they unpacked a crier would roam the streets, announcing their presence. At curtain time residents brought chairs and cushions and settled down to watch Lorca's young actors perform. Lorca used traditional musical instruments like lutes, guitars and vihuelas to accompany his shows. After the performance, the troupe would pack up and store their equipment for the next stop.

In October, La Barraca travelled to Granada to take part in the University of Granada's fourth anniversary celebrations. Federico was very pleased to be in the same theater in which, as a child, he had seen works of the Spanish classics. The members of the group were taken to a performance held in the Gypsy quarter, Sacromonte, and to visit the Alhambra. Later that month, they performed successfully in Madrid's Central University. Critics wrote laudatory reviews of the company's work, acknowledging in particular Lorca's remarkable gifts as director, actor and poet.

In November, the poet again went on a lecture tour, this time to Galicia, then on December 16 to Barcelona to speak about his experience in New York. A critic wrote that the most interesting aspect of Lorca's new style was the persistence of primitive elements of his early works but now applied in a more complex and audacious manner which transformed him from a minor poet into an epic one.

By late December 1932, Federico was back in Madrid where his parents had moved to be closer to their children. Their two sons were by then more or less permanent residents of the capital, and their daughter Isabel had recently begun to attend university there. Only Concha remained in Granada with her husband and two children.

On December 19, 1932, La Barraca gave a special performance of Calderon's *Life Is a Dream* at Madrid's Teatro Español to an audience that included the President of the Republic Alcalá Zamora, Prime Minister Manuel Azaña and other personalities. Keen to impress such an important crowd, Federico spoke of the novelty of La Barraca's work and stressed that he and the other members of the company were acting not from self-interest but for the joy of being able to collaborate in the beautiful honor of a new Spain. The reviews in all the Madrid newspapers were very favorable except for the conservative ones. They were convinced that La Barraca was a propaganda machine serving the interests of Marxists, Jews and Communist agitators determined to bring a Red revolution to Spain.

At the end of December, the travelling group performed in southeastern Spain where in Murcia Federico met a young shepherd-poet, Manuel Hernández, from the town of Orihuela who was finishing his first book. Federico promised him he would do all he could to promote his work in Madrid. Lorca found Hernandez's work to be original and powerful. The year ended brilliantly for La Barraca which justified the faith the government had placed in it. Over the next three years, Lorca would be bound up with the University Theater in whose creation he had played such a critical role.

CHAPTER 12
YERMA – 1934

At the beginning of 1933 two events, one national and one international, dominated the Spanish newspapers: the Casas Viejas massacre and the rise to power of Adolph Hitler in Germany. Casas Viejas was a village in the province of Cádiz where some 500 anarchist laborers, sick of their poverty, proclaimed a libertarian communist revolution. Subsequently they surrounded the barracks of the Civil Guard and in a fray one officer and one sergeant were killed. The government in Madrid immediately issued the order that the rebellion must be put down. On January 12 a large contingent of civil and assault guards arrived in Casas Viejas commanded by a captain who ordered that a house where the anarchists had locked themselves in be set on fire. The rebels died and the next day, the captain executed twelve more men on the suspicion that they had been involved in the attack on the Civil Guard barracks.

The massacre soon became the political controversy of the day. There were rumors by right-wing activists that the order to kill the rebels had been given by Prime Minister Azaña. A full inquiry was ordered and on March 7, he admitted in parliament that there had been illegal executions. The police chief was prosecuted, and the captain sentenced to twenty-one years in prison. Over the next months, conservatives used this tragic episode as a weapon against the prime minister. Meanwhile, with the Great Depression which hit Germany harder than any other country, Hitler rose to power. As chancellor of Germany, he ordered the dissolution of political parties and the persecution of Jews and intellectuals. In Spain the right wing, encouraged by the success of the Nazis, was likewise plotting the collapse of democracy.

At this time, Lorca was preparing the production of *Blood Wedding*. He directed the rehearsals, taking special care over the play's shifts from prose to poetry, making sure to curtail any over-emphasis by the actors and controlling the rhythm of each scene. Federico knew that he had not had any major success in the theater although by this time he was the most famous young poet in Spain. A critic suggested that *Blood Wedding* would be received as the great work Lorca was waiting for. It had to be a success. And he was right. The play scored an all-out hit. Madrid's leading intellectuals, writers and artists attended the first show on March 8, including the Nobel Prize winner Jacinto Benavente, philosopher Miguel de Unamuno and Fernando de los Ríos. The curtain rose on a simple room painted in yellow hues. After the first scene the audience was indecisive in its response, but from the second onwards there was constant applause. The performance was interrupted twice to allow Lorca to take a bow. When the final curtain fell the public went wild and Federico joined the actors on the stage amidst great emotion and joy.

The next day, the reviews were almost wholly favorable although some critics were not happy about the appearance of the moon on stage. Someone pointed out that the moon was the divinity who presided over the poet's poetic universe. It was the mythical moon of the Celtiberians, ancient inhabitants of Spain, who offered up to her their bonfires, dances and songs.

To many viewers, *Blood Wedding* represented a leap forward in the evolution of Spanish theater. Actress Josefina Díaz gave thirty-eight performances before closing her 1933 season in Madrid and then she took the play on tour in the provinces. Throughout the country critics responded favorably to its performances. Lola Membrives, the Argentinian actress, asked if she could produce the play in Buenos Aires. Federico agreed. He felt calm and content because he had the first great triumph of his life with this box-office success. From then on, the poet became financially independent, a victory that for so long had eluded him.

Meanwhile, Spanish fascism, as in Italy and Germany, was on the move. The Falangist periodical *El Fascio* appeared in Madrid. Its publisher's favorite targets were Lorca and La Barraca. One of the collaborators was José Antonio Primo de Rivera, son of the dictator Miguel, who founded the fascist party in Spain. Federico's position on fascism became public knowledge at the time when he joined the Association of Friends of the Soviet Union and signed a protest against the fascist barbarism being perpetrated by Hitler and Mussolini.

José Antonio Primo de Rivera (1903-1936). Spanish fascist founder
of Falange Española. Sentenced to death by the republicans,
he was executed during the first months of the civil war.

At this time, the poet was involved in the amateur club Anfistora which had been founded for the purpose of improving education for women and promoting modern theater. The poet recovered his two plays previously confiscated by the police: *Don Perlimplín* and *The Shoemaker's Prodigious Wife* and in February began rehearsing for their performance at Teatro Español. In April 1933, Anfistora gave a single performance of the two plays. Responses to the productions were mixed. Many reviewers had seen and liked *The Shoemaker's Prodigious Wife* in 1930. But *Don Perlimplín* was new to them. The liberal press by and large praised the work, while right-wing papers attacked it and labeled the play anachronistic. Both pieces deal with the traditional story of a young girl married to an old man. The theme of passion is exemplified in the shoemaker's wife and Don Perlimplín. The former, dreaming of love and of the child she will have one day, also suggests the themes of illusion and of frustration so often an integral part of relationships in Lorca's work. While the two farces are similar in several ways, they have important differences. The mood of *The Shoemaker's Prodigious Wife* is predominantly gay and lively, while the tone on *Don Perlimplín* is dark, mingled with tears, comedy and tragedy, in a powerful foreshadowing of things to come.

After the shows, Federico set off with La Barraca for Valladolid, Zamora and Salamanca while on May 5 the actress Lola Membrives and her company sailed from Barcelona to Buenos Aires to produce *Blood Wedding* in Argentina. Towards the end of June, in a show at the Madrid Residence, Lorca encountered an engineering student who was to become the great love of Lorca's last two years. Born in Madrid in 1912, Rafael Rodríguez Rapún was a passionate socialist who in his position as La Barraca's secretary had gained everyone's respect for his scrupulous rendering of accounts. Meanwhile, Lorca was working on his new play called *Yerma*, a drama about female infertility, but preparations for La Barraca's touring season forced him to interrupt his work on the play that summer.

In Valencia in June the company premiered a new production of *Fuenteovejuna* by Spain's most prolific playwright, Félix Lope de Vega, of the 17th century. Rehearsals consumed Lorca's time and attention as he added popular songs, music and dance to the play that was transparently pro-republican. Lorca condensed Lope de Vega's script so that its focus became not the king and queen of Spain but the country's rural population. His updated staging of the work enraged the right-wing press but Lorca was unapologetic. Workers, keenly attuned to its political implications, greeted the drama with tumultuous applause. La Barraca followed its Valencia appearance with trips to both southern and northern Spain. The company concluded its summer season with an extended stay in Santander. There, the company gave three performances at the International Summer University with some two thousand people attending the opening presentation of three short comic plays by Spain's Shakespeare -- the creator of Don Quixote, Miguel de Cervantes.

Meanwhile, Lola Membrives opened *Blood Wedding* at the Maipu Theater in Buenos Aires on July 29 where it proved so popular that its run was extended. Lorca was ecstatic to hear that the production of the play in Argentina was a huge success. On August 4, he received a telegram assuring him that the play had conquered Buenos Aires and was very profitable. The company was about to set off for the provinces to be back in the capital for more performances by the middle of September, hopefully in the presence of its author. Lola Membrives pressed Lorca to come to Argentina offering to pay his expenses and arrange a lecture series for him. Lorca agreed to make the trip.

Federico left Madrid for Catalonia on September 28 and the following day embarked in the liner Conte Grande for Buenos Aires. Before the ship left Barcelona, Lorca received a letter from Rafael Rodríguez assuring him that La Barraca was hard at work rehearsing a new play. The voyage would take two weeks. On board, Federico managed to write a new lecture and otherwise spent his time reading. During a stop at the Canary Islands, he mailed a letter home to his family as well as a postcard to his friend Rodriguez. A few hours before the liner reached Río de Janeiro, he wrote to his parents about his excitement at arriving in South America. Waiting for Lorca at the quay was the Mexican writer Alfonso Reyes, now his country's ambassador to Brazil, who took Lorca on a brief tour of the city.

After stopping at Santos, the transatlantic docked for a few hours in Montevideo where journalists and photographers went aboard, among them Pablo Suero, a distinguished theater critic who took to the poet and would become one of his closest allies in Argentina. Lorca's vitality amazed him as he appeared old, modern, grave and cheerful simultaneously. On October 13, in Buenos Aires, a crowd of admirers was waiting on the pier when Federico stepped onto the gangplank, suntanned and smiling.

Since the beginning of October, the newspapers in Buenos Aires had been announcing Lorca's arrival, alleging that he was the greatest contemporary innovator of poetry and theater in the Spanish language and there were preparations to hear him lecture and to attend performances of *Blood Wedding* and *The Shoemaker's Prodigious Wife*. The poet stayed in the Hotel Castelar, one of the best in Buenos Aires from where he could watch the crowds passing up and down the street. The hotel was to be Federico's base for most of his stay in the city. In the basement were the studios of Radio Stentor with which he would participate in various broadcasts. Near the hotel was the theater where on October 25 Lola Membrives presented *Blood Wedding*.

From when he arrived in the city, Federico's presence in newspapers and magazines was constant. His success was more resounding than that of any Spanish writer who had visited Buenos Aires before. Within a few weeks he was the talk of the town, and his photograph was shown everywhere. In fact, he was rarely in the hotel as he was constantly invited out. He confided in his friend, Suero, that *The Public* constituted his real theater but that it would never be produced because it was a mirror of the audience revealing what was in each member of the public's mind as they were following the play, and since the inner drama of each of them is often very poignant, members of the public would get up at once in indignation and leave the theater. Rather, Lorca favored a new theater concerned with the problems of contemporary society and wanted to get ordinary working people to be the main audience.

Soon after his arrival Lorca said that he would probably be in Argentina for only one month and a half because he had promised his family to be with them for Christmas. His mother Vicenta was constantly in touch with him by letter or telegram but in the end, it turned out that because of his engagements, his stay would be almost six months.

When Federico arrived in Buenos Aires on October 13 the election campaign in Spain was going on. Later in the month, Jose Antonio Primo de Rivera held the inaugural meeting of his fascist Falange party while various conservative groups merged in an electoral coalition headed by José María Gil Robles, leader of the Catholic party CEDA. The Spanish community in Buenos Aires became divided into two antagonistic camps: the pro-republicans on one side and the monarchists and conservatives on the other. Lorca, questioned by journalists about the situation in Spain, expressed his dislike of the monarchy recalling that the king had left the country in 1931. He said that the coming elections were going to be terrible, and that he was worried about the ongoing political party fights. He also made clear that Spanish conservatives didn't like his work and that in Granada the clergy had a low opinion of his poetry.

On October 20, Lorca gave his first lecture to the members of the Friends of Art Club which was run by a woman of great sensitivity, Elena (Bebé) Sansinena. Federico got to like Bebé and her husband. The reading, *Play of the Duende*, was suited to the audience and showed the poet at his most profoundly Andalusian. The atmosphere in the crowded room was electric, and according to a journalist Lorca conquered the heart of Buenos Aires.

On October 25, Lola Membrives reopened *Blood Wedding* in the Avenida Theater. Before the curtain went up the poet, spoke a few words to the packed house who gave him a standing ovation. The evening was triumphant with the audience enormously impressed, applauding after each scene and urging Lorca to speak again at the end of the play. He was very happy to see that his work had appealed to people from all levels of society, intellectuals and non-intellectuals alike.

Blood Wedding played for several months and generated a huge amount of money for the poet who received ten percent of the takings. He sent his father a check for a large sum to convince him of his viability as a self-supporting writer and to show him that by writing poetry it was possible to make more money than by selling sugar. The day after the opening of *Blood Wedding* Lorca delivered his second lecture and demonstrated his musical ability by singing and playing folk songs on the piano. Following this success, he gave his *New York* recital and finally, on November 8, his *Primitive Andalusian Song*. On November 14, he lectured on *Play and Theory of the Duende* in the Avenida Theater with no seat to spare and later his book *Gypsy Ballads* was published in a special edition in Argentina.

When in Buenos Aires, Lorca frequently met Chilean poet Pablo Neruda who became a good friend. Pablo's father didn't approve of his son's dedication to poetry and Pablo didn't have the support of his mother who had died at his birth. Desperate to escape from his father, Neruda had joined the Chilean diplomatic corps which gave him the opportunity to visit many cities around the world. In 1927 he was appointed consul in Rangoon, Burma. In 1932, he was sent as consul of Chile to Buenos Aires and this is when he meets Federico, who was becoming well known in Argentinian literary circles.

On November 20 Lorca and Neruda attended a lunch given in their honor at the PEN Club. Both poets admired Rubén Darío and decided to talk about the Nicaraguan by devising a speech whose sentences they would deliver alternately from different ends of the table. The poets complained that there was no monument to Darío in Buenos Aires and about the absence of his name on any street or square. They also collaborated in presenting the wife of Argentinian writer Pablo Rojas with a bound typescript of a book of poems by Neruda, illustrated with Indian ink drawings by Lorca which included severed hands, drops of blood, skeletons and the decapitated heads of Lorca and Neruda observed by the eye of a waxing moon. The drawings seem to attempt to stare death in the face and, by doing so, to diminish the terrible power of its grip.

Lorca had some detractors in Buenos Aires; one of these was the writer Arturo Cambours who described his great disappointment on meeting the famous author of *Blood Wedding.* That day, Federico talked non-stop about himself, declaring that Spanish poetry and theater began and ended with him. Cambours declared that he had never seen such pedantry, immodesty and vanity. He described Lorca as a stupid puffed-up fool, a fat and petulant charlatan. Another enemy was Argentinian essayist Jorge Luis Borges who saw the poet as a man acting a part or playing a role, a sort of professional Andalusian.

Meanwhile, in Spain, the country's political situation worsened, with reports of trouble appearing almost daily in the Argentine press. National elections were scheduled to take place on November 19, 1933. At least two political parties were grappling for power: CEDA, the right-wing Catholic alliance, and the Spanish Falange of José Antonio Primo de Rivera, son of the former dictator. Although not a fascist movement altogether, the Falange nevertheless shared goals similar to those of Hitler's and Mussolini's parties. At the Falange's inaugural meeting in October, José Antonio vowed that if the Spanish fatherland were to be maligned, no language but the dialect of fists and pistols would suffice.

Argentine reporters questioned Lorca often about the situation in Spain. Although he tried to appear impartial, he occasionally voiced an opinion. A month before the Spanish elections, he told a reporter that although Spain had a powerful right-wing faction, those who love and enjoy freedom are on the left. For the first time in history Spanish women had been granted the right to cast a vote. In the end, right-wing Catholic and centrist candidates won a majority of seats in parliament while republican nominees lagged far behind. During the next weeks, a new coalition government promptly began dismantling the more progressive programs implemented by former Prime Minister Azaña. The political situation in Spain had deteriorated. While in Argentina *Blood Wedding* continued its triumphant run. Lorca was informed that, because of the conservative win, La Barraca was having difficulties getting its government grant. He was urged to return to Madrid as soon as possible where he was badly needed. Nevertheless, Federico decided to remain in Argentina through Christmas.

On December 1, Neruda attended the opening night performance of Lola Membrives's new production of *The Shoemaker's Prodigious Wife* as a fuller version than the one staged by Margarita Xirgu in 1930. Lorca had collaborated closely with Lola supervising the music. The opening was another huge success and initiated a run of more than fifty performances. Lorca expressed his admiration for Membrives and her company whose enthusiasm made him feel that he was on tour with La Barraca. He had revised his farce substantially for the actress who was now older than the lithe young blonde called for in the original script. Membrives was also a gifted singer and dancer, and Lorca accordingly added five dance sequences to his play. He told a reporter that he preferred the newer, more musical rendition of the play. He delivered the opening night prologue himself dressed in a tuxedo and carrying a top hat in his hand. He spoke to the huge crowd about the magic of theater and released a live dove from his hat. As the bird flew through the house, the audience clapped.

Off stage Lorca was not as successful. He fell in love with an amateur actor who may have been an extra in *Blood Wedding,* asking the young man to accompany him on his jaunts through the city. The romance appears to have lasted only until the actor realized that the poet wanted a physical relationship with him.

News of Federico's successes in Buenos Aires reached Spanish communities throughout Argentina and invitations to lecture flowed in. December 22, he spoke on *Duende* in the city of Rosario. Meanwhile *Blood Wedding* and *The Shoemaker's Prodigious Wife* were doing so well that Membrives asked to produce something else written by Lorca. Both decided to go ahead with *Mariana Pineda* giving a broadcast talk about the play and publishing the story in the newspapers. A few moments before the opening show a basket of flowers with the intertwined flags of Spain and Argentina was delivered to Lola's dressing room. The poet said that he had received a telegram from his parents in Spain in which they asked him to send flowers to the actress. However, the play was far from being a hit and the press commented that it was a mistake to produce this early work of his. Although the audience responded rather well to the production and Lorca was called on the stage at the end of the performance, reviews of the play were, at best, lukewarm describing it as monotonous.

Federico made dozens of drawings in Buenos Aires. Lacking the time and inclination to write, he poured himself into art. On loose sheets of paper, inside books, as an embellishment to his autograph, he drew trailing vines, lemons, flowers, arrows, faces and harlequins. He illustrated poems by his Argentine friends, drawing four pictures of sailors to accompany the Mexican writer Salvador Novo's bilingual *Seamen Rhymes*.

Lola Membrives tried to get Lorca to finish *Yerma*, announcing to the press that she intended to open the company's fall season with the premiere of the play. But first he had to finish the work. He chose Montevideo where Lola and her husband had planned to spend several weeks so that the actress could recuperate from the strenuous Buenos Aires season. He agreed to give two lectures there but because the demand for tickets was so great, he added two more talks to his schedule. The President of Uruguay attended Lorca's first lecture.

Federico spent his time in Montevideo in the residence of the Spanish Ambassador amid receptions, recitals and parties. At a luncheon, he was asked if he planned to marry, and he answered that he belonged to his mother. He always made veiled allusions to his homosexuality.

On February 16 Lorca took the ferry back to Buenos Aires and the following day he wrote home to tell his family about his great success in Montevideo where his lectures had earned him a lot of money. The poet had a compulsive need to prove to his parents that he was capable of being financially independent. He had sent checks to Don Federico and Vicenta encouraging them to spend the money as they pleased. It was his turn to send funds to them in return for those that they had invested in his career.

He made no progress on *Yerma* in Montevideo but did manage to complete an adaptation of Lope de Vega's *The Simple-Minded Girl* which was premiered by Eva Franco at Teatro

Avenida on March 4. The production was a hit, commercially as well as critically and ultimately ran for nearly two hundred performances. The money kept flowing in but the third act of *Yerma* receded further and further into the distance.

Meanwhile, Lola Membrives was performing a program in honor of Lorca: the first act of *The Shoemaker's Prodigious Wife*, the final scene of *Blood Wedding*, the third act of *Mariana Pineda* and a recital by the poet of two scenes from *Yerma*. On March 10, 1934, the newspaper *Crítica* published an interview with Federico on the eve of his departure where he provided some real insights into the sources of his work. When the interviewer brought up the topic of death, Lorca's expression changed instantly as his gaze turned inwards seeming to sink into himself. He explained that he was unable to stretch out on a bed with his shoes on because he was reminded of the corpses he had seen as a child in Fuente Vaqueros.

On March 25 he was still in Buenos Aires. At one-thirty that morning he presented a once-only performance of his newly revised puppet play, *Don Cristóbal's Puppet Show*, at the Teatro Avenida. The production was intended as a farewell gift to the people of Buenos Aires. Fast-paced, loosely structured, and filled with bawdy language, the new show was both an exploration and a defense of creative freedom. Several members of the public took offense at the play's salacious dialogue and blatant sexual allusions. Nevertheless, his success in Buenos Aires and Montevideo had proved to Lorca that his work could attract an international audience. He regarded his experience as a triumph for Spanish theater. In all, Lola Membrives, before returning to Spain the following fall, would perform *Blood Wedding* 150 times, *The*

Shoemaker's Prodigious Wife 70 times, and *Mariana Pineda* 20 times. *The Simple-minded Lady* was shown almost 200 times before the year ended. The poet's visit to Buenos Aires had been an enormous success in every way.

Federico must now face the political situation in Spain that had changed so dramatically since he left the previous October. Before he left for Spain, the poet received an enormous number of presents, including many silver objects, showing the extent to which Lorca had conquered Buenos Aires during his six months' stay. It was particularly difficult for Federico to leave Argentina. On his last night, he begged his friends to pretend the following day that they were only seeing himself off to a nearby place and that they would meet again soon. The following day, March 27, Lorca boarded the liner Conte Biancamano bound for Spain. When the moment of departure came a huge crowd was at the quayside to see him off.

The ship docked briefly in Río de Janeiro where the Mexican ambassador to Brazil presented Lorca with a glass case containing the preserved bodies of half a dozen brightly colored Brazilian butterflies. Five days later, in the middle of the Atlantic, Lorca drafted five new poems.

After a voyage of sixteen days, the liner reached Barcelona and Lorca returned at once to Madrid where he was interviewed and found to have been one of the most effective ambassadors that Spain had ever sent to South America. Federico was also giddy with pride at the enormous amount of money he had made overseas. As for the students of La Barraca, they were jubilant that their director was back at last and that a new period in the life of the company was about to begin.

Lorca was aware of the political situation in Spain where the politician José Calvo Sotelo had founded an ultra-rightwing monarchist group, Gil Robles' Catholic Party was growing more militant and José Antonio Primo de Rivera's Falange was using tactics inspired by fascist ideals. The country was becoming so polarized between liberals and anti-democrats that the situation might lead to civil war. Federico travelled to Granada for Easter where he learned that the local government was acting against the working class. With that in mind, Lorca returned to Madrid to direct a production of *Liliom*, by the Hungarian playwright Franz Molnar, which was shown in the Teatro Español, and to prepare for La Barraca's summer tour to the north. The poet was also trying to finish *Yerma*.

During Lorca's absence in Argentina, La Barraca was being attacked again by the extreme right complaining that the money provided by the government was being squandered on a troupe of homosexual university students. The Falangists accused it of perverting the peasants with corrupt, foreign-inspired customs, shameful promiscuity and an acquiescence to communism.

Since the November 1933 elections, the Spanish government had undergone a number of drastic changes. In the first months of 1934, the coalition government of Prime Minister Alejandro Lerroux repealed a variety of legislative acts imposed by the earlier republican leaders. The new administration restored religious education and payment of priests' salaries, granted clemency to all political prisoners, and abandoned efforts to reform the country's corrupt agrarian system.

In early April, Lerroux abruptly resigned in protest after

the Spanish president delayed ratifying the new act granting clemency to political prisoners. Violent confrontations took place in villages throughout the Spanish countryside. Both right- and left-wing groups began military drills. For many citizens, the specter of Hitler's Germany, where a legally elected, constitutional government was systematically dismantled, loomed large. Spaniards worried in particular about the role the Catholic Church had played in Hitler's rise of power. During the week that Lorca returned to Spain, speakers at a gathering of right-wing Catholic youths in Granada openly voiced their admiration for both Hitler and Mussolini.

On June 1, Pablo Neruda arrived in Madrid on his way to the Chilean consulate in Barcelona, where he had been assigned a diplomatic post. Lorca went to the train station with his companion Rafael Rodríguez and others to greet him. His home became the site of boisterous gatherings that lasted for days. Guests would pack crosswise in bedrooms so that everyone had room to sleep. At a formal presentation later in the year, Lorca introduced Neruda as one of the great Latin American poets of the day. For his part, Neruda thought that Lorca was the guiding spirit of this moment in the Spanish language.

Lorca devoted much of June to La Barraca's troupe, preparing his actors for their weeklong residency at the International University in Santander. In late July the poet returned to Granada to finish *Yerma,* which he did over the next month. At the same time, he began planning his next drama, *Doña Rosita the Spinster,* and composed a number of new poems in which he explored the bonds between birth, death and love.

He called the collection in Arab verse form *The Tamarit Diván*. Tamarit was the name his uncle Francisco had given to his country home, located a few hundred yards from the Huerta de San Vicente. The work gave voice to ideas and images that had absorbed him since childhood. His fascination with the form was part of a widespread revival of interest in Arab culture in the early 1930s in Spain. Although he failed to issue the collection in 1934, Lorca delivered a manuscript to a friend who promised to publish the book under the auspices of the University of Granada. The finished collection numbered twenty poems divided into two roughly equal sections based on traditional Middle Eastern verse forms. Like their ancient Persian counterparts, Lorca's work dwells principally on love, sex and death. The volume as a whole offers a profound meditation on the constant exchanges between the living and the dead, between earth and the cosmos. The *Divan* is both more personal and more erotic that any collection Lorca had written to date. Many poems bear veiled allusions to homosexual love and suggest Lorca's growing desire to acknowledge and to celebrate his sexuality.

Federico returned to Madrid in early August. This summer, two older bullfighters came out of retirement: Juan Belmonte and Ignacio Sánchez Mejías. The latter's followers were worried about his coming back to the ring as he was overweight and had lost much of his agility, but he claimed that he was not afraid of death. After performing at Huesca, he was scheduled to fight at Manzanares to replace Domingo Ortega whose brother had unexpectedly died. After playing his bull in a conventional manner Ignacio sat on the ring's ledge for one of his specialized passes and the bull charged. On a second charge the animal came so close to his body that it slashed the bullfighter's pants. Ignacio tried to get to his feet but failed and was left lying on the sand in a pool of blood.

He asked to be taken to Madrid by ambulance rather than be operated at the plaza's infirmary, but the vehicle was delayed and didn't get into Manzanares until after midnight. The bullfighter arrived in Madrid at seven in the morning of the following day, thirteen hours after the goring, and was rapidly operated on. It was too late. Lorca who was so terrified of death didn't have the courage to visit Ignacio in the clinic. On the morning of August 13, the doctors decided that there was nothing more to be done as the gangrene had spread dramatically. The bullfighter died at 9:45 that morning.

Without seeing the dead man, Lorca left for Santander where he shut himself in with his friends. He was convinced that the matador was fated to die in Manzanares. By the end of October 1934, Lorca was finishing a poem in memory of the bullfighter. In the first part of his *Lament for Ignacio Sánchez Mejías,* Lorca insists that fate had conspired against Ignacio that day, and that Sánchez knew from the moment he announced his return to the ring that this would be his last bullfight. The poem begins with a dramatic description of the struggle between life and death and then covers the human tragedy of the bullfighter in a scenography in which nature participates in the misfortune. Ignacio died nobly, sacrificing his life in a corrida that had nothing to do with sport but rather a religious mystery, the superiority of spirit over matter. It is an elegy that reveals the heroic, pagan, popular, and mystic beauty that exists in the fight between man and bull.

After the death of the bullfighter, La Barraca performances took place in the International Summer School in Santander. The group continued the tour to Palencia on August 25 where, while dining at a restaurant one day, it coincided with José Antonio Primo de Rivera and his friends dressed in business attire. The founder of Falange wrote a note to Lorca written on a napkin saying that together with the actors' coveralls and the blue shirts of his party, they could forge a better Spain. Federico did not respond because the ideals of the Falange and of the democratically-oriented Barraca were completely incompatible.

The tour over, Lorca travelled to Granada where his parents had moved to their summer house in the Huerta de San Vicente. At that time, Federico had finished *Yerma* whose premiere was scheduled for November. Before his return to Madrid there occurred some events that shook the country. On October 1, 1934, the conservative government fell giving Gil Robles cabinet representation, specifically the ministries of agriculture, labor and justice. The reaction of workers and liberals was that the presence of the conservative minister in the government might well spell the takeover of fascists similar to what brought Hitler to power in Germany. Trade unions called a revolutionary general strike for October 4 which was massively supported in the Basque Country, Catalonia and Asturias where miners seized control and prepared themselves to fight to the end.

They resisted fiercely until October 15 when they were finally crushed by units of the Spanish army in Africa which had landed on the northern coast commanded by General Francisco Franco. The repression was brutal with numerous executions and thousands of prisoners taken. Terrorized by the ferocity of Franco's tactics and the cruelty of his troops, particularly the Moroccan units, and demoralized by huge civilian losses, the remaining Asturian rebels surrendered by October 20. Right-wing Spaniards proclaimed Franco the savior of the country and Prime Minister Lerroux subsequently appointed him commander-in-chief of the Spanish armed forces in Morocco.

On October 6 in Barcelona activist Lluís Companys, proclaimed the independence of Catalonia. The separatist adventure didn't last long after military intervention by the Spanish republican army. The Catalan separatist bid played straight into de hands of conservatives. In Madrid, the Falange called for a massive general demonstration outside the Ministry of the Interior. For José Antonio Primo de Rivera the sacred unity of Spain was being threatened by a marxist conspiracy organized by Moscow, and it was the duty of every Spaniard to resist this threat. The battle lines were clear: Spain had plunged into a bitter struggle between republican and nationalist forces, left and right, communists and fascists.

Lorca remained in Madrid throughout the crisis. The repression in Asturias by the army horrified him and he voluntarily spoke out against the bloodshed that had occurred in northern Spain.

Someone asked Lorca why La Barraca was not putting on any plays. Federico responded by saying that they couldn't perform when there were so many widows in Spain. Towards the end of October, *Yerma* was finished and on November 4 the poet gave the first reading of the work to a group of friends who viewed the elegy as a masterpiece. At this time,

Margarita Xirgu was rehearsing to produce the play at the Teatro Español and Lorca was working on his play titled *Doña Rosita the Spinster* which he described as a piece 'of gentle ironies of tender caricature, imbued with the charm and delicacy of past periods when the nightingales really sang, and the gardens and flowers were topics for novels.' In the play, Federico was exploring his own specific time past as well as the spirit of the Granada that had made him the poet he would become.

His own life was now somehow compartmentalized. With close friends he was open about his sexuality; with his family he was evasive. He enjoyed numerous liaisons as he needed lots of sexual adventures but he was discreet and knew whom to approach when and where. However, he was aware that despite the more tolerant atmosphere of the republic, hatred of homosexuals ran deep in Spain. One right-wing newspaper published a diatribe against homo-sexual men who had corrupted Madrid by inflicting their vice on innocent young men. The article called for the ar-rest of such reprobates.

In mid-November *Yerma*, the second of the rural trag-edies, began rehearsals in Madrid with Margarita Xirgu in the title role. The play reflected the atmosphere of suffoca-tion, vigilance and envious gossip common at the time in the rural world. A young woman who lives the calamity of her sterility expresses her inward suffering to her coarse husband. While he views her as a sexual object, she thinks of him as the father of a child that doesn't materialize. The female protagonist suffers a sort of feminine hysteria be-cause of her obsession with maternity. She could perhaps become a mother by yielding to local males who pester her but she doesn't because of her moral duty as a wife. The tragedy ends when Yerma strangles her husband. She shouts tragically "I have killed my son."

The origin of this play reaches back to the poet's childhood, when he was aware of the people's pilgrimage to the village of Moclín in search of fertility. It is possible that Federico had a real person in mind as the protagonist. One candidate may have been his father's first wife who died childless. About the play, the poet explained that Yerma was a victim of the Spanish code of honor as she had made the fatal mistake of marrying a man she did not love preventing her from looking for a more suitable partner. It is a rejection of the rigidities of Spanish Catholicism as conservatives quickly realized when the play was later produced. There is also a rejection of male chauvinism, which relegates women to the category of second-rate citizens belonging only in the bedroom and the kitchen. The reactionary press, however, without exception refused to acknowledge the author's talent but claimed instead that his work was immoral, anti-Catholic, irrelevant to Spain's problems and lacking in veracity. Garcia Lorca's name was by now firmly affiliated with liberalism and, in the event of a right-wing revolution, his love for Granada would be no guarantee of his safety in the town.

A major theme in *Yerma* is that of honor, for it is partly the protagonist's belief in honor that keeps her from adultery and faithful to an uncaring husband. The author considers the concept of honor to be virtue and moral rectitude. Also, the name Yerma is linked to the soil, to nature, and the relationship between men and women and the natural world, and is as much a central theme in the play. It is precisely in her awareness of herself as part of the barren, unproductive processes of nature, and in consequence, of her isolation from its beauty and abundance that Yerma's tragedy lies. Her physical sterility becomes the emotional and spiritual emptiness of despair, the richness of her spirit pitifully withered. By the play's conclusion, Yerma is the one who conveys its real meaning, the sense of the pain and pointlessness of human life.

The dress rehearsal of *Yerma* was December 28 and the premiere the following night with the theater fully booked. From the upper gallery extreme right attendees began hurling insults at Margarita Xirgu calling her a lesbian and at Lorca calling him a homosexual. The rest of the audience reacted indignantly, and the hecklers were expelled from the room. The performance continued amid rising enthusiasm for the quality of the work and for the excellence of acting and the sets. When the final curtain fell the applause was deafening and Lorca, calm and confident, took his bow. Federico and Margarita were overwhelmed.

Nevertheless, the right-wing press were unanimous in their condemnation of the play which they considered immoral, anti-Spanish, irreligious and an implicit rejection of Catholic values, especially when the Old Pagan Woman asserts that she doesn't believe in God. The widespread disdain for Lorca by many conservative Catholics dated from the premiere of *Yerma*. Federico was now seen as an enemy of the Church by conservatives although liberal minded people thought that the play had brought a breath of fresh air to Spanish theater. Critics found the play to be realistic, clear and sincere marking a step towards liberation from medieval backwardness and oppression. A Catholic daily included *Yerma* on a list of shows that readers should refrain from seeing. The paper claimed the drama was crude, disrespectful and overly sensual. Officials in Granada banned the presentation of the play during Corpus Christi celebrations arguing that the work's moral content would be particularly offensive to the local population during an important Christian holiday.

CHAPTER 13
DOÑA ROSITA THE SPINSTER – 1935

Lorca was now working on *The Destruction of Sodom* which he described as an audacious work with a grave and compromising title, but he would draft only fragments of the play that would never be finished. However, emboldened by the public's response to *Yerma,* Lorca announced shortly after the start of the new year that he was about to complete the third section in his trilogy of Spanish tragedies.

The year 1935 marked the tricentennial of Lope de Vega's death, an event widely celebrated by the Spanish theater community. Lorca spoke of the classic playwright with veneration, describing him as a man of national tradition. He saw himself as a spiritual and aesthetic heir to Lope, writing plays exalting Spain's historical and cultural patrimony, and in the process participating in the creation of a second Spanish Golden Age. To help launch the country's yearlong observation of the tricentennial, Federico collaborated in the production of one of Lope's plays. It opened on January 25 with the attendance of dozens of prominent critics. In a speech to the opening-night audience, he called for renewal of the greatest traditions of Spanish theater. By costuming the cast in authentic peasant clothing from the Spanish countryside of 1935, he hoped to bring the atmosphere of Lope's play nobly and peacefully to life. He had spent days scouring the region of Castile for both old clothes and old songs with which to animate the production.

At the end of January, the actors and actresses of Madrid requested that Margarita Xirgu give a special after-hours performance of *Yerma* so they could see it. Xirgu agreed and gave an actors-only presentation at one-thirty in the morning. Thunderous applause erupted the moment the curtain rose and Margarita had to wait for the sound to die down before starting the play. The crowd clapped at the end of each act and gave the cast a standing ovation at the final curtain. Moments later, Lorca spoke to the audience from the stage. He told the crowd that for some time he had rejected homages, tributes, and testimonial dinners in his honor but he had agreed to accept this tribute because it came from his peers and especially to make the case for a theater of social activism. He wanted to continue fighting for artistic freedom as long as he lived.

However, taken to a different culture in the United States, Lorca's work was not so well received. Irene Lewisohn, co-founder and director of the Neighborhood Playhouse in New York City, premiered the first version of *Blood Wedding.* Lewisohn had approached Lorca two years earlier for permission to produce the tragedy. Under the title *Bitter Oleander,* the play opened in New York on February

11 with caustic reviews as Lorca's lyrical Andalusian drama fell on uncomprehending ears. Both audiences and critics found Weissberger's stilted translation laughable. A critic ridiculed the play, despite what he conceded were moments of considerable poetic virtuosity. He described the stage set as a theatrical interpretation of an old Spanish intestinal tract. Nevertheless, a few American critics perceived the work's merits. The *New York Sun* called it an intense and moving drama. *The New Republic* hailed Lorca's poetic mind and his deceptive simplicity, but the critic warned that the play was hopelessly far from Americans' experience. Lorca acknowledged the beastly things the New York press said about his play, but insisted his work had not failed totally with the public.

Meanwhile in Spain, *Yerma* continued to enthrall the public and to prompt debate. On March 12, Xirgu and her company celebrated the hundredth performance of the play. Ultimately it ran for an impressive 150 performances before closing on April 20, 1935.

Lorca continued working on the play *Doña Rosita the Spinster* whose theme was, according to the poet, the tragic aspect of social life of those Spanish women who never find a husband. This play is a middle-class comedy focusing on the epoch of Federico's parents. Now, the rural tragedy of his previous plays is changed to a provincial drawing room drama. The same as Yerma, Doña Rosita is a middle-aged woman's long painful monologue. In the play, the protagonist has a boyfriend when she is young but when they are about to get married, he decides to travel to America. All her life, Rosita awaits a letter that never arrives and as time passes, the sorrow becomes nostalgia, a faraway recollection, a slow pain that destroys one by one her hopes of ever marrying. Lorca shows the audience the dreams of the protagonist and the changes that occur as years go by. The play is a profound history of psychological pain that develops in three separate epochs, the first in 1885, when the hopeful Rosita is twenty years old, the second in 1900 as a childless middle-aged woman, and the third in 1911 in which the protagonist shows her virtuous dignity until the end. Lola Membrives announced plans to premiere the play but Lorca did not offer it to her as she had hoped. Nevertheless, she did present *The Shoemaker's Prodigious Wife* and *Blood Wedding*. The critics were enthusiastic writing that the Membrives' versions were a revelation.

Lorca had now three plays in theaters in the capital. This meant prestige as well as cash, so he could face the future confidently as he was earning more money than ever. Reporters speculated correctly that he was one of the season's most financially prosperous playwrights, but Federico was indifferent to his earnings, insisting that success would not shackle him and he would always work as he had up until then. He thought that money was sometimes useful, but not always, and that glory was a vague thing that deluded people who dream of having it, but that usually brings only bitterness and sorrow.

Lorca spent Easter in Seville as the guest of the keeper of the Arab castle of the Alcázar. His host installed a piano in the garden near the house where the poet played Spanish folk songs. Federico lived his visit to Seville intensely observing the processions and being entertained by local Gypsies. Back in Madrid, the republican government feared that a right-wing coup might occur at any moment, especially after

Gil Robles became minister of war and strengthened the army to oppose a possible marxist revolution. He appointed young General Francisco Franco, who had a reputation as an enemy of democracy, as his chief of staff. In the following months, Gil Robles carried out a harsh purge of known liberal and left-wing officers in the army, all of which added fuel to the fire. In fact, it was felt that Gil Robles supported the restoration of the monarchy within the framework of a fascist-style state.

Lorca's fifth rendition of *Gypsy Ballads* sold out immediately and it was announced that the sixth had gone to press. The poet's work was seen now as an interpretation of the mystery of life and of man at the deepest levels.

On May 23, it was announced that Lorca's new play *Doña Rosita the Spinster* was completed. The play was relevant to contemporary Spain. The work was set in a typical *carmen* of Granada that looked across the valley to the Alhambra and the slopes of Sierra Nevada, the Granada that Federico knew so well as a child and adolescent and from tales told by his mother. *Doña Rosita* is a work that expresses Lorca's complex relationship with Granada, a town that he both loved for its culture and beauty and feared for its intolerance and resistance to change. The play would open later on December 13 at the Teatro Principal Palace in Barcelona with the cast headed by Margarita Xirgu as Rosita and directed by Cipriano Rivas. The work was reviewed as having been written by an author who combined his great talent as a poet with his outstanding gift as a dramatist.

In May 1935, Prime Minister Lerroux formed a new cabinet that included five members of CEDA. His CEDA-dominated government worked to further dismantle the reforms Manuel Azaña and his administration had put in place, and to purge loyal republican officers from the ranks of the Spanish army. By the summer, conservative government forces had prevailed in their long-standing efforts to cut government spending for La Barraca, and the troupe lost much of its funding. Lorca defended his company. He said he intended to do only one thing about the dire financial situation, go on performing to ensure La Barraca's survival.

In the months leading up to the electoral victory of the Popular Front, the members of the Granada right thought of Federico as the queer with the bowtie. After their victory months later, they would grow even more vicious.

On June 28 and 29 Margarita Xirgu put on classic Lope de Vega's *Fuenteovejuna* and *El Alcalde de Zalamea* in the Palace of Charles V in the Alhambra in Granada. The following month Federico returned to Madrid and read *Doña Rosita the Spinster* to Xirgu at a hotel in the Gredos Mountains near the capital where the actress was taking a brief vacation. She was impressed with the script and planned to begin her season in Barcelona in September with *Yerma* and produce *Doña Rosita* in October, after which the company would spend a few days in Italy and sail for Mexico in November.

On August 19, La Barraca's performances began in Santander, but the poet complained that its financing had been cut in half when conservatives came to power and that somewhere more money had to be found. Also, if conservatives tried to prevent them from erecting their stage, they would act in the streets and squares of villages. Anything rather than give in. However, from this summer on, Lorca, increasingly engrossed in his own work, began to distance himself from the group which had elected new representatives to the committee to run the theater.

Meanwhile, Margarita Xirgu and her company reached the village of Fuenteovejuna to discover that authorities had imprisoned a local anarchist specifically so that he would be unable to attend her performance of the play named after this town in which tumultuous events from 300 hundred years ago regarding a lecherous military commander are portrayed. Lorca joined Xirgu in announcing to the town that the show would not go on unless the anarchist was freed. The mayor yielded and the man was released. During the final curtain call, audience members were so moved by the work and its call for liberty that they rushed the stage demanding unity in the quest for liberty. Lorca worried about the extreme right. The commander in the play is the archetypal bully for whom women are mere objects. It was the mentality of conservative, intransigent males that Lorca was combatting in his literary work. He knew only too well who his enemies were.

The following day, the poet visited Córdoba where a newspaperman asked Lorca why he was so obsessed with death. Federico responded that he couldn't help it. He felt like a glow-worm on the grass terrified that someone was going to step on him. On September 8, Margarita gave a final performance at Teatro Español in Madrid and left for Barcelona with Federico.

At the end of September Lorca and Salvador Dalí met after seven years without seeing each other. On the 28th both artists went to Tarragona, fifty miles south of Barcelona. Lorca was exhilarated to be with Dalí again and Salvador's wife Gala was as delighted with Federico, and the poet was intrigued by her. Here was a woman capable of satisfying Dalí. Salvador praised the dark and surrealist ideas that filled Lorca's *Yerma* and proposed that they work together, so the two made plans to collaborate on a project that both would write and design, that never transpired. After a few months their friendship again slackened.

On October 6, Lorca gave a public reading to commemorate the first anniversary of the Asturian revolution. Sponsored by the Barcelona Atheneum and held in a crowded theater, the event was broadcast over radio and aimed specifically at the workers of Catalonia. For the reading Lorca sat onstage behind a table with a huge microphone. The moment he began to speak the packed auditorium fell silent. He read two of his works. When he finished the crowd jumped up and shouted, "Long live the poet of the people." He marveled at those who had come to hear him: artisans, old workers, mechanics, children, students. The event was bound to provoke his opponents, but he didn't care. In a nation so torn by political, religious, and social discord as Spain was in 1935, no public figure could escape accusations of partisanship.

Lorca's reading to commemorate the Asturian revolt coincided with news of the Italian army's invasion of the African nation of Abyssinia, the first step by Mussolini toward creating a new Roman Empire. Because of the Abyssinian invasion, Margarita Xirgu cancelled her planned Italian tour and announced that she would extend her company's season in Barcelona to include a new production of *Blood Wedding,* while Federico condemned what he described as the tyranny of fascist regimes in Italy and Germany. He declared his solidarity with artists in both countries.

On October 23 Margarita Xirgu performed *Fuenteovejuna* in the Teatro Olympia theater, the proceeds of which were to be distributed among the political prisoners still in jail because of the revolutionary events of recent years. When the performance ended, the audience threw hundreds of red flowers on to the stage. Margarita wept, deeply moved by the display of Catalan fervor. Shortly afterwards Federico returned to Madrid, where the Radical Party was implicated in a scandal over a government license awarded for a fraudulent variant of the roulette wheel which was to be introduced in Spanish coffee houses. Conservative Gil Robles sought to use the case for his own ends, no doubt hoping to take control of the cabinet, but internal dissension within his own party prevailed opening up the possibility of a general election.

On October 26, Xirgu began a short season in Valencia with *Yerma*. Lorca arrived from Madrid for the last performance before Margarita left the city. A journalist asked him several questions raising the issue of the vulgarity of the play which had offended certain people. Federico admitted that he intended to provoke his audiences. The poet said that in theater now there were two topics that interested people: social problems and sex and that he preferred to write about sex. Critics in Valencia raved about the play and audiences praised the work. On closing night, a wildly enthusiastic crowd filled the theater, and Xirgu received floral bouquets from two local republican associations.

A young acquaintance of Lorca's travelled from Barcelona to Valencia to see *Yerma* and found the poet impatiently awaiting the arrival from Madrid of a friend and expressing his anxiety in two sonnets scribbled on sheets of notepaper bearing the heading of Hotel Victoria where he was staying. Lorca probably referred in the poems to intimate friend Rodríguez Rapún, the athletic, handsome mining engineer, who was a member of La Barraca and who would join him a few days later. The sonnets become part of a larger collection of poems about a love affair between two unnamed persons and range in tone from the mundane to the exalted. Together they speak of a troubled, at times cruel relationship between two partners, one of whom is more blindly devoted than the other, and consequently suffers more. In writing the sonnets Lorca was careful not to disclose the gender of his protagonists but in them the author uses a masculine past participle to describe his beloved, indicating that their affair was homosexual. Later, Lorca referred to the eleven poems as *Sonnets of Dark Love,* possibly meaning love without destination, without future. Lorca seems to have written his *Sonnets of Dark Love* with one person in mind: Rafael Rodríguez Rapún.

After Valencia, Margarita Xirgu and Federico returned to Barcelona to prepare for the opening of *Blood Wedding* which was scheduled for November 22. He composed new music for several scenes and accompanied the production on the piano himself. Midway through rehearsals, Rodríguez joined Lorca in Barcelona. One night, after listening to flamenco music, Rodríguez left with a Gypsy girl and failed to return to the hotel where he was staying with Lorca. Federico was in despair believing that Rafael had abandoned him. He explained to his friend Rivas Cherif that he had been attracted to men since childhood. According to the poet, his close relationship with his mother made it impossible for him to feel heterosexual passion. While his brothers and sister were free to marry, he belonged to Vicenta.

Lorca was delighted with Margarita Xirgu for her part in *Blood Wedding* that opened in Barcelona. The play's sets seemed to him magnificent, while he accompanied on the piano. The piece was a hit and the critics were almost unanimous in their praise of the production.

Lorca, however, was concerned with the forthcoming production of *Doña Rosita the Spinster* that was to premiere on December 12. As rehearsals proceeded and the date for the opening night approached the excitement grew. One newspaper wrote that no opening of a play had ever aroused such expectation and that during these days there were only two topics of conversation in Barcelona: *Doña Rosita* and the country's political situation. The government had fallen at the beginning of the month. The moderate Manuel Portela Valladares would head an interim government at a time when a general election was inevitable.

Doña Rosita staggered the audience that packed the Principal Palace and the critics didn't fail to notice that far from being a comedy, the play was essentially a tragedy that induced lips to smile and hearts to grieve. Lorca had achieved a miracle by making people laugh and cry at the same time. At the end of the second act, the audience gave the cast a standing ovation. Lorca and his actors had to go on stage eight times before the crowd quieted down. Within a week *Doña Rosita* had received more than twenty-five reviews. Although some critics questioned the work's genre and style, nearly everyone praised the originality and power of Lorca's script. By Christmas Eve the play was the most successful spectacle in Barcelona.

Federico's last days in Barcelona included dinners in his honor, excursions with his friends through the medieval quarter and a multitudinous banquet in the Inglaterra Hotel that was attended by the best Catalonia artists and intellectuals. Lorca thanked his hosts in an extemporaneous speech and recalled his childhood maids who had proved such an inspiration to him as a writer. He then returned home for Christmas. The town of Fuente Vaqueros sent New Year's greetings to Lorca. The mayor and nearly fifty residents of the village signed a note applauding his achievements and acknowledging him as the true poet of the people.

Meanwhile, Italy continued the invasion of Abyssinia and Hitler increased his belligerence in Germany. The fear of a new conflagration was spreading across Europe. In Spain, sessions of parliament had been suspended until January 1, 1936, the president dissolved the assembly and the date for general elections was set for February 16. Then came the end of press censorship and the newspapers detailed accounts of what had happened in Asturias, Catalonia and the Basque Country. There were still thousands of political prisoners and the clamor for their release grew day by day. Rumors were circulating about the formation of an electoral Popular Front to face conservatives at the polls, while conservatives and fascists allied to create a National Front.

Lorca left for Madrid on December 24. On January 6 Margarita ended her successful season in Barcelona. It had been three very good months for the poet and actress, impossible to forget.

Two years after losing the elections in November 1933, the left decided to avoid making the same mistakes as the February elections approached. In the summer of 1935, the Communist International had opted for a policy of collaboration with the democratic parties and now signed an agreement creating a Popular Front based on the return of the religious and educational policies of the first two years of the republic that called for efficient and rapid agrarian reform and amnesty for the political prisoners still in jail because of the insurrection of 1934. The five weeks of the electoral campaign were tense; Gil robles was presented by the conservatives as a sort of Spanish Mussolini who would save the country from the threat of a red Revolution. The Falangists had already begun to prepare themselves for the civil war which they thought was imminent. Violent clashes went on as Spain divided increasingly into two antagonist camps with less and less room for moderates in between. Lorca, who had grown more radical in his views, threw his lot in with the Popular Front while his parents expressed their anxiety about the outcome of the polls.

PART 5

Death of Lorca

Que muerto se quedó en la calle
que con un puñal en el pecho
y que no lo conocía nadie.

And he was left dead in the street
with a dagger in his breast
and no one knew him

CHAPTER 14
LA CASA DE BERNARDA ALBA – 1936

Lorca returned to Madrid in January talking of his recent triumphs in Catalonia and future plans for both travel and work. He had promised to accompany Margarita Xirgu on an extended tour to Cuba, Mexico and South America that year. The actress intended to leave Spain and head first to Cuba, where she would present *Yerma*. Lorca planned to meet up with her overseas. Meanwhile he immersed himself in work. In late December he brought out *Six Galician Poems*, followed by *Blood Wedding* and *First Songs*, a small compilation of early works. Within the next few months Federico hoped to debut his volume of sonnets as well as a collection of *Old Spanish Songs* and *The Divan of Tamarit*, a book of poems of Arabic influence.

By early January he was still wrestling with his projected collection of New York poetry and he had begun work on a new play, a drama about a serious social problem in which theatergoers would participate directly in the action. Federico planned to call it *The Dream of Life*, a political tragedy linked to the Asturian miners' rebellion. The work is the most blatant of Lorca's efforts to incite a confrontation between stage and audience. Lorca proudly described the first act of the play as completely subversive which assumes a veritable technical revolution, an enormous advance. With *The Dream of Life*, Federico hoped to create a bona fide peoples' theater stripped of artifice and devoted to truth. The second act was to take place in a mortuary, and its final scene in a heaven filled with Andalusian angels.

Lorca made a brief visit to Saragossa to see the actress, Carmen Díaz, whom he had decided would be the best person to produce the revised version of *The Andalusian Puppets* which had been set to music. At the end of the month, Federico was with Margarita Xirgu in Bilbao where they gave a joint recital. On January 31, Margarita sailed for Havana and would never see Federico again.

On the political front, by the start of 1936, the Second Republic was in the midst of its twenty-sixth governmental crisis. Internal squabbling and two massive financial scandals had discredited the administration of Prime Minister Lerroux, forcing him from office in the fall of 1935. To settle the crisis, President Alcalá Zamora dissolved parliament and called for general elections to take place in February. The country's left-wing parties set aside their differences to forge a Popular Front.

Young intellectuals were in favor of the Popular Front. Poet Rafael Alberti was one of them. He had just returned to Spain from a long visit to South America and Russia and was given a lunch in his honor at the Café Nacional in Madrid. During the meal, Lorca read for the gathering's approval a statement in support of the Popular Front which was published in the communist daily *Mundo Obrero* the day before the elections with his own name at the head of more than 300 signatures. The article appealed to the common sense of voters and expressed the signatories' conviction that only through a united effort on the part of liberals could the country recover the idealism of the first years of the republic. There could be no doubt about Lorca's commitment to the cause of democracy, and during the following months his position was confirmed with widespread publicity in the press.

On February 14, two days before the election, Rafael Alberti organized a Popular Front function in the Zarzuela Theater in honor of the controversial novelist and playwright, Ramón María del Valle-Inclán who had died on January 5. Lorca participated in the program by reading an extract from the prologue to one of Valle-Inclán's plays and two sonnets by Rubén Darío dedicated to the writer.

On Sunday, February 16, Spain went to the polls. The results gave the Popular Front a victory with the republican coalition obtaining 267 votes of parliamentary representation against 132 of the conservatives. Republicans were euphoric and the first decision by the new government was to free political prisoners. However, the failure of Gil Robles to win the election had a shattering effect on his followers, many of which shifted their allegiance to the Falangists. The Popular Front's victory had terrified the wealthy, who imagined that a marxist revolution was just around the corner. From February onwards, with provocations, assassinations and retaliations from both sides, the picture grew increasingly grim. The Falange mounted a direct-action campaign with the specific goal of creating chaos and making a right-wing coup in the name of law and order inevitable.

On February 19, Manuel Azaña assumed power again as the new prime minister of Spain. He maintained an official state of alarm throughout the country with strict press censorship. He signed a general amnesty for all political prisoners and a series of military postings were issued. It included orders that Francisco Franco be removed from his government post as chief of staff and go to the Canary Islands to serve as commander general. Franco viewed the posting as banishment, and his resentment of the republic would evolve into aggression. The general began talking openly of his admiration for Mussolini.

In the weeks following the elections, members of the left staged parades in Madrid and other large cities. In Granada, massive demonstrations by both conservative and liberal groups took place. Proponents of the radical left set fire to Catholic and right-wing institutions. On March 9, members of the Falange went on the attack in Granada; they disrupted classes at the university medical school, skirmished with antifascist protesters, and fired on a crowd of workers. Several citizens were wounded. The local trade unions retaliated by calling a general strike. Citizens burned the Falange headquarters, the offices of a conservative newspaper, the building of the local Catholic party, a theater and two cafés.

Manuel Azaña Díaz (1880-1940). Spanish prime minister of the Republic and organizer of the Popular Front prior to the civil war.

On March 14, several Falangist leaders in Madrid were arrested. Four days later the organization was outlawed, making matters worse. The Popular Front government imposed a state of emergency, which gave the police special powers. More and more the situation was coming to be seen in terms of crude opposition between fascism and communism with young right-wing militants joining the Falange and the left-wing ones joining communist and socialist organizations.

Amid all this, Lorca continued to make his liberal position clear, reading his poems at a mass meeting, and joining the Association of Friends of South America and the Friends of Portugal, founded with the aim of informing the Spanish public about the fascist regime of Portugal's dictator Oliveira Salazar. On April 5, Lorca gave a radio talk about Granada's Holy Week verbalizing his objections to recent innovations which made Easter celebrations more brash and noisy. He went on to say that Granada was still divided into two incompatible halves.

Two days later a Madrid newspaper published an interview with the poet in which he referred to his current obsession with theater which, according to Federico, had an absolute duty to immerse itself in the problems assailing humanity. Lorca was now determined to see *Doña Rosita* produced the following season in Madrid by Margarita Xirgu who was still in South America. Referring to his work in progress, Federico said that he was writing a new play with a religious and socio-economic theme stating that as long as there was economic injustice in the world, people would be unable to think clearly, and that the day when hunger is eradicated will be the greatest spiritual awakening the world has ever seen. He was talking like a real socialist. From a Spanish right-wing point of view Lorca, by April 1936, was just short of being a communist.

On April 20 Lorca attended the presentation of a book of poems by Luis Cernuda where Cernuda spoke about giving poetic form to his predicament as a homosexual in an uncomprehending and intolerant society. Meanwhile, La Barraca was in Barcelona to commemorate the coming of the Republic in 1931 but Lorca was not with the group, having distanced himself definitively from the University Theater. In its four years under Federico's leadership, the group had put on nearly two hundred free performances of classic Spanish plays in towns, villages, and cities throughout the country and it grieved Lorca to part from the troupe. Now, he plunged into his own theater work.

The theater club Anfistora wanted to premiere his *Once Five Years Pass* in Madrid in July 1936. The poet had completed the script almost five years earlier and, although he considered the play to be unproduceable, he allowed the club to stage the work and even took an active part in the rehearsals. He sat in the hall, his script on his knees, deleting lines that didn't work. When he realized the protagonist's death at the end of the play was lasting longer than it should, he crossed out the last eight lines of the script. However, in June he abruptly canceled the production saying that he preferred to wait until fall to premiere this theatrical piece. In fact, he feared premiering the potential controversial work in such politically troubled times.

Not one to rest idle, Lorca wrote another play, a more commercially viable tragedy in the same vein as *Blood Wedding* and *Yerma*. It was intended to be a drama of sexuality set in Andalucía. Federico called the play *The House of Bernarda Alba* and noted that the work should resemble a photographic document. In an effort to simulate the effect of photography he set the play in black and white, with the exception of one costume, a green dress worn briefly in the third act. He hoped to produce *The House of Bernarda Alba* in the fall of 1936, with Margarita Xirgu in the title role.

On May 1 the United Socialist Youth Movement held a demonstration to show the fascists what they were up against. Despite having supported the Popular Front, the socialist party refused to participate in the new government, wasting its energies in what was practically a civil war within its own ranks. In the meantime, conservatives were conspiring in the dark while Lorca continued to side with the workers in their demands for better conditions. His message, published in a communist magazine, to all workers of Spain was that they should be united by the desire for a more just and fraternal society. During the city's May Day celebrations, he was spotted in Madrid waving a red tie and shouting his support for the working class.

La Casa de Bernarda Alba (written in 1936). Drama by Federico García Lorca about women in an Andalusian village in which a matriarch wields ruthless control over her five daughters.

Along with political tension, violence was increasing throughout the country. On May 7 the extreme right killed a republican officer known to be one of the instructors of the socialist militia. The following day, an attempt was made on the life of Prime Minister Alvarez Mendizábal who had made insulting remarks about the army. The funeral of the republican officer turned into an angry political demonstration with insults, clenched fists and demands for revenge. On the political scene, Manuel Azaña asked Casares Quiroga to be prime minister although Casares was the wrong man for the job. He was too stubborn, arrogant and aggressive.

On May 29 a newspaper published in its theater page the rumor that in eight days Lorca expected to finish the last of his rural tragedies, *The House of Bernarda Alba*, but in fact Federico would not finish the much-anticipated play until three weeks later. The play, with women only, is set in an arid Andalusian village. The plot was inspired by a woman who lived with her family next door to Federico's cousin, a woman known to be a pretentious, despotic widow, wielding a cane as a weapon to abuse her servants, her mother and especially her daughters. For Lorca the family served as a metaphor for rigid, intolerant, hypocritical Spanish Catholicism concerned more with appearance than humanity.

Following her second husband's death, Lorca's Bernarda condemns four of her daughters, dressed always in black, to seclusion at home for the traditional eight years of mourning their father. An oldest daughter by Bernarda's first marriage, Angustias, is allowed to become engaged to a rakish gallant known as Pepe el Romano whom all the daughters find attractive, but especially the youngest, Adela. Although Pepe prefers Adela and has furtive, passionate encounters with her, he prefers even more the father's inheritance that will come with marriage to Angustias. When Bernarda discovers the affair between Adela and her sister's fiancé, she becomes infuriated with defiant Adela who breaks her mother's cane, symbol of demonic power. Bernarda confronts Pepe el Romano with a gun and shoots as he flees on horseback, missing him. Hearing the shot and thinking him dead, Adela hangs herself. As a servant takes the body down, Bernarda remarks coldly, "Tell them she died a virgin,"

The House of Bernarda Alba reveals the atmosphere of a small Andalusian village, the pitiless heat of summer, the arrival of reapers in the village, incredibly long periods of mourning, women relegated to the house, spying, hidden behind curtains, anticipating sexual scandal. Bernarda, with her hypocrisy, her inquisitorial Catholicism and her determination to suppress other people's freedom, represents a mentality known only too well to the poet. Lorca saw conservative Spain as always ready to crush the vital impulses of people like Bernarda's daughters and servants. Raised among kindly women, Lorca deplored their inferior status in society and the assumption that men deserve greater privilege, education and freedom.

Lorca wrote this play depicting despotism at a time when everyone knew that there was a real possibility of a right-wing coup in Spain. The poet was probably influenced by his father, Don Federico García, as he was the only powerful landowner in his vicinity who professed democratic, republican ideas. He was disliked because he paid his men better than the others did and even went so far as building houses for them. Don Federico was the good landowner of the village while Bernarda Alba was precisely the opposite. In the play, Adela affirms her absolute right to her own sexuality, and she sees her determination to be her authentic self in terms of Christian sacrifice. When the family discovers that she not only loves Pepe el Romano but that the relationship has been consummated, her reaction contains a clear allusion to the crucifixion. It reflects the poet's conviction that the day we stop resisting our instincts we'll have learned how to live.

The play would be produced for the first time at the Teatro Avenida in Buenos Aires in 1945 by Margarita Xirgu and her theatrical company. Its success was immediate and a few days after the performance a bronze plaque in memory of Lorca was unveiled in the foyer of the theater. In following years, the *House of Bernarda Alba* was to be presented in many of the world's major cities.

On June 10 in a newspaper interview, Lorca was asked his opinion of the fall of Moorish Granada to Ferdinand and Isabella in 1492. He said that it was a disastrous event in which an admirable civilization, a poetry, architecture and sensitivity unique in the world were lost. Lorca's comments quickly became known in the city where they infuriated many who believed that the fall of the Moorish kingdom was a great Christian victory over paganism, paving the way to the country's unification and the conquest of the New World. The poet trod on many conservative toes when he said that he was totally Spanish but that he hated anyone Spanish who, just because he was born a Spaniard, with a blindfold over his eyes demeans himself for an abstract, nationalistic ideal.

The poet continued to give readings of *The House of Bernarda Alba* and became more enthusiastic about what he had accomplished with the play. One night, Federico was dining with some friends when Fernando de los Rios talked about the Popular Front falling apart and fascism growing rapidly, which meant that the situation was deteriorating fast. There were rumors concerning a military conspiracy against the republic that Prime Minister Casares was refusing to take seriously, believing that if there were an uprising it would be put down as easily as the one headed by General Sanjurjo in 1932. Lorca was in a somber mood, anxious about increasing violence that was gripping Madrid. On June 2 the National Confederation of Workers (CNT) and the socialist General Union of Workers (UGT) brought out builders and electricians for a strike that went on for some time. The Falangists themselves were inciting violence. Shots were heard more frequently. Lorca showed a friend where a stray bullet had come through the window of his apartment. Trembling, he remarked that it could have killed him.

Federico was in a quandary worried what would be next. Was there going to be a military coup? What should he do? Finally, he decided to leave Madrid and go to Granada although his friends told him that he would be safer in Madrid than anywhere else. He was also advised that if he wanted to leave the capital, he should go to Biarritz rather than to Granada.

On the evening of June 12, the situation in the city became explosive when a group of gunmen assassinated Lieutenant José Castillo of the police. Castillo, a militant anti-fascist had been a marked man for months, receiving numerous anonymous threats. In the early hours of the following morning, his friends carried out an appalling reprisal, kidnapping and shooting conservative politician José Calvo Sotelo, leader of the extreme-wing opposition in Parliament, and dumping his body in the municipal cemetery. Calvo Sotelo was the martyr conservatives needed, and his death provided the opportunity because, thanks to the participation in it by uniformed men, it could be presented as a crime perpetrated by the state. Calvo Sotelo's murder was used later to justify the rebellion although, in fact, plans for it were in place well before his brutal death.

By late June, Lorca was still toying with the possibility of a trip to Mexico, where Margarita Xirgu was enjoying a triumphant tour. The last weeks of June and first week of July brought strikes by trade union members, elevator attendants, waiters, even bullfighters. Political murders took place almost daily. On July 2 two Falangists sitting at a Madrid café were shot and killed by a gunman in a passing motorcar. Later that day right-wingers sought revenge by murdering two presumed members of the left. Lorca grew more and more fearful. Left alone in his family's seventh-floor Madrid apartment, he yielded to old fears and superstitions. He became so petrified by the violence that gripped the city that he rarely went out except in the company of close friends. At approximately nine in the evening on Sunday, July 12, four Falangists murdered a leftish member of the assault guard in Madrid. That same night, Lorca gave his last reading of *The House of Bernarda Alba* and told friends that he would never be political but that he was a revolutionary. The assassination of Calvo Sotelo had cast a black shadow over Lorca's disposition. It's likely he felt that the end was near.

Lorca's parents had returned to Granada a few weeks earlier so he decided to join them there without delay. After having lunch with a friend on July 13, both took a taxi to the outskirts of Madrid to have a quiet brandy and to discuss the situation. Lorca asked his friend what he should do but finally made up his mind to get to Granada by July 18, his and his father's saint's name day. (The day recognized for the saint a person is named after is more significant in traditional Spain than a person's birthday). At the train station, his friend helped to install Federico in a sleeping car where a Granada government official was also travelling. To Lorca the coincidence of the official being there was a bad omen. He was afraid.

The poet arrived the following morning in the Huerta of San Vicente. Doña Vicenta wrote to her daughter Isabel to say how delighted she was to have Federico with them. There he was reassured to find his parents, his sister Concha, his piano and his oaken writing table.

During his first days in Granada, Lorca read *The House of Bernarda Alba* to some friends and got to work on *The Dreams of My Cousin Aurelia,* which he hoped to complete that summer. He had begun the script earlier in the year and planned to premiere it in the fall. The work takes place in Fuente Vaqueros. The play is an elegy to provincial life, an homage to the days when human existence still yielded to fantasy and dreams, before the advent of the machine age with its factories and engines. Set in 1910, the play belonged to a sequence of so-called Grenadian Chronicles that began with *Doña Rosita the Spinster* and was to continue with a work called *The Nuns of Granada.* Lorca based the work's protagonist, Aurelia, on a cousin he had known and loved as a child. He completed a single act of the work, much of which is a long and comic exchange between Aurelia and three other women, who read and discuss a novel as if its characters are close personal friends.

On July 14, 1936 Granada was the scene of constant disturbances, provocations and strikes, since the February elections. Although the conservatives had won the elections, the results were debated with the Popular Front alleging that serious fraud had been committed on polling day. The results were officially annulled and a fresh election was called for. The outcome was inevitable with right-wing members of the population abstaining massively. The Popular Front won an overwhelming victory without a single conservative candidate being returned. Deprived of parliamentary representation, the Granada upper class swung further right, and support grew for the anti-republican conspirators who were now completing their plan for the downfall of the republic.

In the city, the small but determined Falangist party had grown even stronger after the electoral failure of Gil Robles' coalition in February and even more powerful when the Granada results were abrogated. The Falangists thought that the days of the Republic were numbered and that the Popular Front would be overthrown by the joint action of the army and themselves. The Falange now incited a nationwide wave of street violence and prepared for civil war as confrontations with trade unions made life in the city increasingly tense. Following a massive left-wing demonstration, two churches were destroyed, the premises of the Catholic daily newspaper wrecked, the offices of right-wing organizations pillaged, and the Catholic theater gutted. The Falange, socialists, communists and anarchists were ready to take up the arms.

At this time, the Granada Falange operated in liaison with the rebels in the army garrison whose commandant José Valdés Guzmán was a fanatical enemy of the Republic. Three days before Lorca returned to Granada, a new military governor arrived in the city. General Miguel Campíns was known to be a friend of General Franco but turned out to be a staunch republican, so the right couldn't count on his support for the uprising. The new civil governor of the province, César Torres, refused to distribute arms to the workers and when the moment struck, he would prove unable to act decisively to stop the rebel movement.

On his arrival at the Huerta de San Vicente, Lorca was delighted to find that a telephone had just been installed. He soon called his old friend Constantino Ruiz Carnero, editor of the newspaper *El Defensor de Granada*, who announced on the front page of the daily that the great poet had just arrived in the city to spend time with his family. Federico's return was also printed in the city's other two newspapers, so now it was certain that the conspirators were aware of the poet's presence in Granada. In fact, he was often seen in town enjoying his celebrity status with his fellow citizens. Some of these might have been aware of Lorca's allusion in an interview in Madrid to Granada's upper class which he declared was the worst in Spain. That interview caused a considerable stir in the city and did nothing to enhance the poet's reputation among those who at that very moment were finalizing their plans for an assault on Spain's democracy.

CHAPTER 15
THE MILITARY
UPRISING – 1936

On July 17 the feared anti-republican revolt began in Spanish Morocco and the following morning General Franco broadcast a message from the Canary Islands announcing he would attack the Republic. Meanwhile in Madrid, the Prime Minister Casares Quiroga declared that the government was in control of the situation, but General Queipo de Llano turned traitor in Seville by usurping the command of the garrison. By nightfall, Queipo had taken the center of the city and was preparing an assault on working-class quarters. He used the powerful radio station in the city to harangue the conservative audience and threatened republicans with extermination if they did not surrender.

Troops from Morocco landed in Cádiz and Algeciras on the southern coast of Spain and Franco issued a declaration of war demanding that the legitimate republican government in Madrid surrender or be bombed. In Granada, the civil governor obeying orders from Prime Minister Casares refused to accede to the demands of left-wing organizations that arms be distributed to the people. That night Casares resigned, and his successor Martínez Barrio still withheld the order to distribute the weapons while his efforts to form a governing coalition floundered. Franco's political supporters, the Falange, began to fill the streets. That morning, panic, fear and rage seized the Madrid working class who demanded that arms be made available. A new government was finally formed under former Minister of the Navy José Giral with full left-wing representation and the explicit task to arm the people at once.

The order to distribute weapons was not transmitted immediately to Granada, where confusion reigned at every level and the local government believed that the garrison would remain loyal. The mayor of Granada was a young socialist, Manuel Fernández-Montesinos, married to Lorca's sister Concha. He kept the family informed of what was happening in the city, telephoning them at Huerta de San Vicente.

By dawn of July 18 nationalist troops under the command of Francisco Franco had taken control of Las Palmas, the capital city of the Canary Islands, and declared martial law. At 5 A.M. Franco issued a declaration denouncing foreign influences in Spain and threatening war without quarter against the politicians in power. For its part, Radio Madrid announced later that morning that absolutely no one on the Spanish mainland had taken part in the absurd plot, and that the uprising would quickly be quelled. But even as the broadcast was being read, army garrisons throughout Andalusia were mobilizing against the government.

Friends and family members dropped by the Huerta de San Vicente all day long on the eighteenth to pay their respects to Lorca and his father on their saint's day. Federico had talked about conservative congressman Calvo Sotelo's murder earlier in the week and admitted that he was worried. Meanwhile, the communist leader Dolores Ibarruri came on the air from Madrid and urged citizens to resist the rebellion. Women, she said, must prepare to fight the insurgents with knives and boiling oil. Ibarruri's closing words became the rallying cry of the left: "*No pasarán!*" (They shall not pass!). Later that night both the president of the republic and the prime minister resigned and appointed Diego Martínez Barrio in their stead, with the expectation that he would strike a deal with the rebels rather than fight them.

In Granada, the local radio station continued to broadcast government exhortations from Popular Front spokesmen, while from Radio Seville came reports of national victories all over the country. The next morning Granada received the confirmation that Queipo de Llano was indeed in control of Seville. The Nationalists had seized Burgos, Zaragoza, Pamplona, Valladolid, and Segovia. In the south, troops from Africa began arriving to shore up the existing nationalist stronghold in Seville. Republicans held on to Madrid, Valencia and Barcelona. The Spanish Civil War had begun.

On the afternoon of July 20, the Granada garrison, commanded by two colonels and a captain, finally rose. General Campíns was arrested at gunpoint by his own officers whom he had trusted and was forced to sign the proclamation of war. At 5 P.M. the troops left their barracks and without opposition took the main official buildings in the city. Civil Governor Torres was apprehended in his office, as well as Mayor Fernández-Montesinos, Lorca's brother-in-law. Within an hour most of the Republic's authorities were arrested and imprisoned and the whole town occupied except for the Albaicín working-class quarter. There, trenches were dug to prevent access to vehicles and barricades put up to block entrances to the narrow pedestrian alleys. It took three days for the rebels to control the area.

The city's cafés and bars filled with men in uniform: army, Falangists and Civil Guardsmen. Former members of the civil government, republican partisans and prominent members of trade unions were arrested and jailed by the hundreds. The city's first executions took place July 21, one day after the nationalists seized Granada. By July 23, the whole of Granada was in the hands of the insurgents although they knew that their position was far from secure because the city was surrounded by republican territory and counterattacks might be launched at any moment. To eliminate any possibility of renewed resistance from within, the rebels strengthened Granada's defenses by establishing a reign of terror in the city. There were daily executions of left-wing prisoners against the wall of the cemetery by assassination squads operating with impunity, butchering and reducing the population to a state of absolute panic. Army Commander José Valdés assumed the post of civil governor and telephoned all mayors throughout the province ordering them to hand over their authority to the local Civil Guard. By the morning of July 23, 1936, white flags hung throughout the Albaicín and a total surrender followed. The nationalist victory in Granada was complete and the city went silent.

On July 25, General Orgaz arrived by air with orders from General Franco to supervise plans for the defense of Granada. He counted on the help of one artillery and one infantry regiment under the command of General González Espinosa. The military immediately started a brutal repression by tracking down and shooting any defiant republican. At the civil government building, Commander Valdés was surrounded by a group of civilian Falangists who tortured prisoners by hanging them from the ceiling by their wrists, and they shot people in the cemetery. The Falange enlisted about 2,000 recruits during the first days of the uprising to help with the running of the city's essential services and to denounce all those who were 'opposed to the fatherland.' Valdés also gave free rein to groups of killers called the Black Squads, a loose collection of individuals who enjoyed carrying out executions without a trial.

As soon as the town fell to the rebels, lists began to be drawn up of those considered enemies of the new regime. Condemned men were herded into prison where they spent the night and at dawn they were roped or wired together, bundled into trucks and driven to slaughter. Intellectuals, lawyers, doctors and teachers were among the executed, along with huge numbers of left-wing supporters. On July 29, republican planes bombarded Granada for the first time. Many civilians perished in the attack.

The Lorca family was anxious about the fate of Concha's husband, Fernández-Montesinos, mayor of Granada, who was still in jail. Soon the family themselves had first-hand experience of fascist violence. On August 6, a Falangist squad arrived at Huerta de San Vicente and searched the premises. The following day, a young architect, friend of the poet, appeared at the Huerta trying to escape. Don Federico promised him that that night some peasant friends of his would take him to the republican zone, only a few miles away. Just then an ominous car approached down the lane and the architect dashed behind the house to hide under the bushes. That night, the young man crossed republican lines to safety.

On August 9, things took a turn for the worse when an armed group arrived at the Huerta looking for the brother of the caretaker wrongly accused of having killed two people on the day the uprising began. The men searched the farmer's house and pushed his mother down the stairs as she kept insisting that she didn't know anything. Then they tied the terrified caretaker to a tree and beat him with a whip. Federico, who was witnessing the scene with his parents and sister, could stand it no longer and rushed forward to protest the farmer's innocence. The poet was thrown to the ground and kicked. One member of the group recognizing Lorca said that he was the little queer friend of Fernando de los Ríos. Federico protested that he was the friend not just of the socialist professor, but of many people of different backgrounds. There was no doubt that the attackers knew exactly where his political sympathies lay. They warned him that he was under house arrest and that he must on no account leave the premises.

Lorca was now frightened thinking that next time they might come for him so he ought to seek refuge. He thought of his friend the young poet, Luis Rosales who had also returned to Granada just before the trouble began in July. Two of Luis's brothers were among the town's leading Falangists.

Federico immediately telephoned Rosales and told him what had happened. Rosales promised to go at once with his brother Gerardo. Federico explained to his friends that thugs had roughed him up and had gone through his private papers. The two men discussed the options available to Lorca, including getting him into the republican zone but Federico said he preferred to go to their home.

Before leaving, Rosales warned the family that on no account must they reveal Federico's whereabouts. The Rosales' house was just 300 yards from the civil government headquarters where Valdés was busy organizing the repression, but the large property appeared to be a haven of security. The home was a typical Grenadian house with an interior patio and a marble staircase leading to its upper floors. Lorca was given a bedroom on the third floor of the house. He felt an overwhelming sense of relief.

The Rosales' father had built up a thriving hardware shop in the city and so was one of the best-known merchants in town, respected for his kindness and integrity. He was a liberal conservative in politics with little time for the Falangists, but his wife approved of the fervor of her two other sons, José and Antonio, for the Falange in which they were active officers.

Soon after his arrival, Lorca relaxed and slipped into a routine of reading, piano playing, and conversation while attended by Mrs. Rosales, her daughter Esperanza, Aunt Luisa and a female servant. When Luis Rosales returned home late at night, still clad in his blue Falangist uniform, he and Federico often talked of poetry and about Lorca's forthcoming collection of sonnets. The two also spoke of composing an anthem to the Spaniards who had perished in the fighting that summer. Lorca volunteered to write the music if Rosales would draft the lyrics.

Luis Rosales, a liberal conservative like his father, had little option but to don the blue Falangist shirt and before long he was promoted to positions of some importance having to spend most of the day out of town. His father, by agreeing to shelter the poet, behaved with considerable bravery and magnanimity at the time when it was strictly forbidden to protect a red. As events turned out, the Rosales patriarch would end up paying a hefty price for the privilege of having done his best to protect the poet from his enemies.

Lorca could not possibly write under such conditions and spent much of his time reading the local newspaper which Esperanza took up to him each morning, and listening to the radio, both republican and rebel. Federico learned the full horror of what was happening including the executions taking place daily in the cemetery. According to Esperanza, the poet occasionally talked to his family by phone and begged the Rosales to do everything in their power to intervene on his brother-in-law Montesinos' behalf, but shortly before sunrise on August 16, he was shot in the cemetery along with twenty-nine other prisoners.

The terrible news reached Federico who was shattered and feared for his sister and her three children. If the rebels were capable of shooting people as innocent as Montesinos, how could a poet considered to be a red hope to escape?

Lorca got the answer on August 15 when a group arrived at the Huerta with a warrant for his arrest. The leader of the band threatened his family saying that if they did not reveal the whereabouts of the poet, his father would be taken away instead. Terrified, Concha blurted out that

Federico had not escaped but was staying at a house of a Falangist friend who was, like him, a poet. Now the pursuers knew where he was hiding. The enemy moved fast. They looked for Lorca first at the house of Luis' brother, Miguel, and realizing their mistake soon located him.

On the afternoon of August 16, a car with three uniformed officers pulled up to the Rosales' house while armed soldiers stationed themselves along the street and on neighboring rooftops. Federico was arrested and taken away by order of Governor José Valdés. The person who arrived at the house to detain Lorca was well known in Granada, an ex-member of the local parliament, Ramón Ruiz Alonso, who had belonged to Gil Robles' right-wing Coalition Party and now was a member of the Black Squad. Pompous and pugnacious, he loathed Fernando de los Ríos and there are indications that for Lorca he felt a mixture of scorn and envy describing him as the poet with the big head.

None of the Rosales family members were at home at the time. Mrs. Rosales stood up bravely to Ruiz and stubbornly refused to let him take the poet away, but he stated categorically that the poet was in trouble because of what he had written. Mrs. Rosales then tried to contact her sons by telephone, eventually locating Miguel at Falangist headquarters and telling him what was happening. Rosales was amazed when he entered his street to see that the area had been cordoned off by police and militia. Ruiz told Miguel that Lorca was a Russian spy and that he had done more damage with his pen than others with their guns. His orders were to escort Federico to the civil government headquarters.

At the moment of the apprehension, Federico was trembling and wept. He was wearing dark grey trousers, a white shirt with a loose tie, and had his jacket over his arm. Ruiz Alonso led him out the door and around the corner to a waiting vehicle. In the car, Lorca implored Miguel to intervene at once on his behalf with the authorities and to contact his brother José who he knew was one of the most important Falangists in Granada. On the second floor of the government building Lorca realized that something serious was taking place while Miguel Rosales was hoping to sort the problem out with the governor, but Valdés was not there. In charge was a retired military officer of the Civil Guard who explained that the governor was visiting the front outside the city and was not expected until that evening. In the meantime, he took charge of Lorca. Miguel tried to calm Federico, promising that he would be returned as soon as possible to his brother José and assuring him that nothing bad would happen to him. However, Rosales was extremely worried fearing that the poet might fall into the hands of one of Valdes' brutal accomplices who might torture him. After being searched, Federico was locked in one of the rooms on the first floor of the building while Miguel went back to the Falangist headquarters looking for José. He couldn't find him, Luis or Antonio, all of whom were at the front.

When Luis and José Rosales arrived in Granada that evening, they were outraged to learn what had happened. They decided to confront Valdés who had not yet returned. They were asked to make a formal statement concerning the matter. Luis met directly with Ruiz and asked him how he had dared to go to his house to arrest his guest. Ruiz answered that he had acted on his own initiative and left the room. In Luis Rosales' statement, he declared that Lorca was threatened in his own house, that Lorca had requested his help, that he was politically harmless and that, as a poet himself, he couldn't refuse to help a person who was being unjustly persecuted and that he would do the same thing again.

Later that evening José Rosales went to the civil government headquarters and began a violent discussion with Valdés. The governor told him that he had a typewritten accusation against the poet drawn up and signed by Ruiz Alonso stating that Lorca, a subversive writer, had a clandestine radio in the Huerta de San Vicente with which he was in contact with the Russians, that he was a homosexual, that he had been the secretary of Fernando de los Ríos (which was not true), that the Rosales brothers were betraying the movement by sheltering a notorious red (although he was never affiliated with the Communist Party). Valdés insisted that it was his duty as governor to verify the accusations. Meanwhile he promised that nothing would happen to the poet. After the discussion with Valdés, José Rosales saw Lorca briefly and gave him his word that the following morning he would come and take him away. He then drew up a carefully worded exculpatory statement in which he gave his reasons for protecting Lorca. He hoped that such a procedure would help not only the poet but the Rosales family as well.

When Ruiz Alonso took Lorca away, Mrs. Rosales telephoned the poet's family who had moved into their daughter Concha's apartment. Don Federico set off in search of a lawyer to defend his son thinking that there would be a trial with the possibility of a legal defense. The trial never took place.

The following morning José Rosales obtained from the military command an order for Lorca's release and hurried with it to the civil government building. Valdés told him that it was too late, that Federico had been taken away. The governor, concerned about an adverse reaction against the nationalist cause for killing the poet, contacted his superior General Queipo de Llano to ask for his advice. Queipo recommended Lorca's execution. Even so, the person most responsible for the poet's death was Valdés because he could have granted a reprieve for Lorca if he had wanted. From Valdes' point of view, Lorca was a repellent red, his work was subversive, and his private life disgusting. Federico had also attacked Granada's Catholic upper class, the very people who were now supporting the rebellion.

Lorca was taken from the civil government building on August 18 handcuffed to another victim, an elementary school teacher and staunch republican who had fallen afoul of the secretary of his local municipality who, when the war began, denounced him as a dangerous individual. He was arrested at his home by a group of Falangists and taken to the jail in Granada. A witness saw Federico coming out of the civil government building surrounded by guards and Falangists who pushed Lorca and the others into the truck that was to drive them to their place of execution. The seven men drove through Granada in the dark, to the northeast edge of the city and turned onto a bumpy road that snaked sharply up into the parched foothills of the mountains.

During the two and a half days that Federico spent in prison in the civil government headquarters, several people tried to intervene with Valdés on his behalf. One of them was composer Manuel de Falla. He was told that the poet had already been shot.

CHAPTER 16

THE POET'S LAST
HOURS – AUGUST 1936

Six miles from Granada lie the villages of Alfacar and Víznar. The latter, converted into one of Granada's rebel fortified outposts, was known because it was a nationalist execution site. In July 1936 José María Nestares, a young captain who was in charge of that military position, was in constant touch with Valdés. Every night vehicles would arrive from civil government headquarters with groups of people targeted as undesirables to be shot at dawn. Above the village, where the ground levels out, spread the broad expanse of the *vega* with the stark Sierra de Elvira whose treeless slopes form a harsh contrast with the lushness of the plain. A watercourse runs beside the road and there stood a building which served as a makeshift prison which every night received trucks filled with condemned men and women. A party of freemasons and other prisoners was brought here to dig the unmarked graves for the victims.

That fateful evening, a car stopped before an old building that had been turned into a nationalist command post. After a short wait, Lorca and his companion were driven to a red stone house just below Víznar, at the edge of a ravine. Soldiers, guards, grave diggers, and a pair of housekeepers occupied the upper floor. Lorca asked for confession but the priest had already left. The prisoners were locked in a downstairs room until the early morning. Shortly before dawn, Lorca, the school-teacher and two bullfighters known for their left-wing politics were taken out and shot on an empty stretch of hillside flecked with olive trees. The gravediggers would bury them in the morning.

The exact location of Lorca's body has never been determined. There is a road that winds on around the valley in the direction of Alfacar. A slope of clay and pebbles stretches steeply up a hillside towards the first rocky outcrops of the sierra. Shallow graves were dug in the slope and the bodies tossed in with a thin layer of stones and soil thrown over them. That night, the truck stopped not far from a spring of water known as the Big Fountain. It was here, just before reaching a pool, that the victims were shot, leaving their bodies beside an olive grove on the right-hand side of the road coming from Víznar. This is the ravine where the bodies of most victims lie.

After the execution, one gravedigger reported that he recognized the two bullfighters, the schoolteacher and the young man wearing a loose tie. He helped bury them on top of each other in a narrow trench beside an olive tree. According to accounts, the poet was not killed instantly by a rifle shot so he was finished off with a handgun. Later that morning in Granada one of the members of the firing squad boasted that he had fired a bullet into his ass for being queer. It was August 19, 1936. Federico was 38 years old.

Meanwhile, the music composer Manuel de Falla was trying to intervene on the poet's behalf by getting a few young Falangists he knew to go with him to the civil government headquarters. He found the place packed with people and sat down on a bench while one of his companions went to make inquiries. He was told that the poet had been taken away that morning. That same day, a member of the fascist militia turned up at Lorca's house with a note scrawled by Federico that read, 'Father, please give this man a donation of 1,000 pesetas for the army.' Don Federico, believing that by paying he could save his son, handed the money over to the man. Those were the last words written by the poet. His father carried the note in his wallet until he died nine years later in New York.

Before Lorca was shot the morning of August 19, at least 280 people had been killed against the cemetery walls, while burial records for the three years of the war listed 2,000. Seen in the context of the repression of Granada, the poet's death was no more exceptional than that of university professors, town councilmen, doctors, teachers, and the thousands of humble workers and trade unionists who were murdered throughout the province. The rebels were determined to liquidate all their left-wing opponents, and Lorca was considered to be just one more red.

It was about three weeks before the republican press picked up the rumor that Lorca had been killed by the fascists. The news was verified when several people escaped from Granada and told the story of what was happening in the city with convincing information about the poet's arrest and death. There was outrage throughout the Spanish-speaking world. Federico had been executed in his beloved Granada. Almost overnight Lorca became a republican martyr.

Margarita Xirgu was in Havana, performing *Yerma*, when she learned of Lorca's death. That night she changed the ending of his play so that Yerma's final cry 'I myself have murdered my child' became 'They have murdered my child.'

Franco's triumphant nationalist soldiers marched into Madrid on the morning of March 27, 1939. Three days later, the last remaining republican strongholds fell to Franco's army. Four decades of dictatorship followed. The winners of the war never accepted responsibility for Federico's death.

At the end of 1939, months after the war ended, Lorca's family started proceedings to have his death officially entered in the civil register. Two witnesses found by Granada authorities swore that they had seen his body lying by the roadside between Víznar and Alfacar, and in 1940 a certificate was issued stating that the poet died in the month of August 1936 from war wounds. His body has never been found.

The surviving members of the Lorca's family, parents, brother Francisco and two sisters left Spain at various points during and shortly after the war and were reunited in New York in 1940. Francisco García Lorca married the daughter of Fernando de los Ríos in 1942 and taught Spanish literature at Columbia University and Queens College. Lorca's brother longed for an early end to Franco's dictatorship, and a prompt return to Spain, but it was not to be. Franco's cold hands let go of the reins of power only with his death in November 20, 1975.

PART 6

Selected Poems

FROM BOOK OF POEMS

Lorca's work *Book of Poems* was printed in June 1921 with a dedication to his brother Francisco. The book offers the poet's memories of his days of childhood and youth. One critic emphasized that the poems are too sentimental which in his view marred much of the work but that Lorca was on his way to becoming a genuine poet of the avant-garde. Federico commented that if in the book he had not yet found himself, he felt that he is on the right path 'of daisies and multicolored lizards.' In fact, the author shows that his writings were gaining maturity with beautiful lyric passages at this formative stage of his poetry. He was creating a new aesthetic without losing contact with the traditional. It was a real attempt to renovate Spanish poetry. He was looking for how to express himself personally, mixing what was popular with what was traditional, in an effort to create his own voice. Sensual and elegiac, *Book of Poems* is the work of a gifted but immature writer.

!Cigarra! – Cicada!
August 1918

¡Cigarra!	Cicada!
¡Dichosa tú!	Happy cicada!
Que sobre lecho de tierra	On a bed of earth
mueres borracha de luz.	you die drunk with light.
Tú sabes de las campiñas	You know from the countryside
el secreto de la vida,	the secret of life,
y el cuento del hada vieja	and the tale of that old fairy
que nacer hierba sentía	who could hear the grass be born,
en ti quedóse guardado.	a secret you kept.
¡Cigarra!	Cicada!
¡Dichosa tú!	You are fortunate!
Pues mueres bajo la sangre	For you die under blood
de un corazón todo azul	of an all-blue heart.
La luz es Dios que desciende,	The light is God descending,
y el sol,	and the sun,
brecha por donde se filtra.	the slit it filters through.
¡Cigarra!	Cicada!
¡Dichosa tú!	Happy cicada!
Pues sientes en la agonía	For you feel in your agony
todo el peso del azul.	all the weight of the blue.

Todo lo vivo que pasa
por las puertas de la muerte
va con la cabeza baja
y un aire blanco durmiente.
Con habla de pensamiento.
Sin sonidos…
Tristemente,
cubierto con el silencio
que es el manto de la muerte.

Mas tú, cigarra encantada,
derramando son te mueres
y quedas transfigurada
en sonido y luz celeste,

¡Cigarra!
¡Dichosa tú!
Pues te envuelve con su manto
el propio Espíritu Santo,
que es la luz.

¡Cigarra!
Estrella sonora
sobre los campos dormidos
vieja amiga de las ranas
y de los oscuros grillos,
tienes sepulcros de oro
en los rayos tremolinos
del sol que dulce te hiere
en la fuerza del estío,
y el sol se lleva tu alma
para hacerla luz.

Everything alive that passes
through the doors of death
goes head down
with a white sleepy air.
With thoughtful speech.
Soundless…
Sadly,
cloaked in silence
that is the robe of death.

But you, bewitched cicada,
die releasing song
while being trasfigured
in sound and celestial light.

Cicada!
Happy cicada!
You are wrapped in the robe
of the Holy Spirit itself,
who is the light.

Cicada!
Singing star
over sleeping fields
old friend of the frogs
and of shadowy crickets,
you have golden tombs
in the turbulent beams
of the sun that wound you
in the vigor of summer
and the sun carries off your soul
to make it into light.

Sea mi corazón cigarra
sobre los campos divinos.
Que muera cantando lento
por el cielo azul herido
y cuando esté ya expirando
una mujer que adivino
lo derrame con sus manos
por el polvo.

Let my heart be a cicada
over heavenly fields.
Let it die singing slowly
wounded by the blue sky
and as it fades
let a woman I forsee
scatter it with her hands
on the dust.

Y mi sangre sobre el campo
sea rosado y dulce limo
donde claven sus azadas
los cansados campesinos.

And let my blood on the field
become sweet and rosy mud
where weary peasants
dig their hoes.

¡Cigarra!
¡Dichosa tú!
Pues te hieren las espadas invisibles
del azul.

Cicada!
You are fortunate!
For you are wounded by invisible swords
from the blue.

FROM POEM OF THE DEEP SONG

This work had many reviews, among which were those saying that Federico digs down deeply to the very bedrock of eternal Andalusia. In the book, Lorca expresses his profound knowledge of the Flamenco singing of Andalusia. He knew that *cante jondo* resonated a deep well of emotion and anguish. The origin of this type of song can be traced to Arabic melodies, some say, or to echoes of Jewish canticles in their synagogues. The essential characteristics of this poem are Andalusian, expressing the deepest feelings of the soul of the land, a sadness emerging from the wildest of solitudes.

Federico García Lorca

Poem of the Deep Song
Written in 1921 – Published in 1931

Dos muchachas – Two girls

<u>*La Lola*</u>   <u>Lola</u>

Bajo el naranjo, lava   Under the orange tree, she is washing
pañales de algodón.   cotton diapers.
Tiene verdes los ojos   She has green eyes
y violeta la voz   and a violet voice.

¡Ay, amor,   Oh love,
bajo el naranjo en flor!   under the orange tree in bloom!

El agua de la acequia   The water in the ditch
iba llena de sol.   flowed full of sun.
En el olivarito   In the small olive grove
cantaba un gorrión.   a sparrow was singing.

¡Ay, amor,   Oh love,
bajo el naranjo en flor!   under the orange tree in bloom!

Luego, cuando la Lola   Later, when Lola
gaste todo el jabón   uses up all the soap,
vendrán los torerillos   the young bullfighters will come.

¡Ay, amor,   Oh love,
bajo el naranjo en flor!   under the orange tree in bloom!

<u>Amparo</u>

Amparo,
¡qué sola estás en tu casa
vestida de blanco!

(Ecuador entre el jazmín
y el nardo.)

Oyes los maravillosos
surtidores de tu patio,
y el débil trino amarillo
del canario.

Por la tarde ves temblar
los cipreses con los pájaros,
mientras bordas lentamente
letras sobre el cañamazo.

Amparo,
¡qué sola estás en tu casa
vestida de blanco!

Amparo,
¡y qué difícil decirte:
yo te amo!

<u>Amparo</u>

Amparo,
so alone in your house
dressed in white!

(Equator between jasmine
and nard.)

You hear the marvelous
fountains of your courtyard
and the faint yellow trill
of the canary.

In the afternoon you see
the cypresses tremble with birds
while you slowly embroider
letters on the canvas.

Amparo,
so alone in your house
dressed in white!

Amparo,
and how difficult to say:
I love you!

FROM SONGS

This book contains light and simple verses, with a musical intonation in the lullabies and children's songs from the poet's land. Some of the poems can be described as astral, profound, with complex insinuations hidden in simple songs.

Songs
1923

Nocturnos de la Ventana – Nocturns from the window

1

Alta va la luna.
Bajo corre el viento

(Mis largas miradas,
exploran el cielo.)

Luna sobre el agua.
Luna bajo el viento.

(Mis cortas miradas
exploran el suelo.)

Las voces de dos niñas
venían. Sin esfuerzo,
de la luna del agua,
me fui a la del cielo.

2

Un brazo de la noche
entra por mi ventana

Un gran brazo moreno
con pulseras de agua.

1

High rides the moon.
The wind blows low.

(My long glances
explore the sky.)

Moon over the water.
Moon beneath the wind.

(My short glances
explore the ground.)

The voices of two little girls
drew near. Without effort,
from the water's moon,
I went to that of the sky.

2

An arm of the night
comes in through my window.

A great swarthy arm
with bracelets of water.

Sobre un cristal azul
jugaba al río mi alma.

On blue crystal
my soul was playing river.

Los instantes heridos
por el reloj ... pasaban.

The instants wounded
by the clock ... were passing.

3

3

Asomo la cabeza
por mi ventana, y veo
cómo quiere cortarla
la cuchilla del viento.

I lean out of my window,
and I see
how the wind's blade
wants to cut it off.

En esta guillotina
invisible, yo he puesto
las cabezas sin ojos
de todos mis deseos.

In this invisible guillotine,
I have placed
the eyeless heads
of all my desires.

Y un olor de limón
llenó el instante inmenso,
mientras se convertía
en flor de gasa el viento.

And a scent of lemon
filled the immense moment,
as the wind became
a flower of chiffon.

4

4

Al estanque se le ha muerto
hoy una niña de agua.
Está fuera del estanque,
sobre el suelo amortajada.

In the pond a water girl
died today.
She is outside the pond,
shrouded on the ground.

De la cabeza a sus muslos	From her head to her thighs
un pez la cruza, llamándola.	a fish passes, calling her.
El viento le dice "Niña,"	The wind calls out "Child,"
mas no puede despertarla.	but cannot wake her.
El estanque tiene suelta	The pond has unwound
su cabellera de algas	its hair of long algae
y el aire sus grises tetas	and the wind her gray breast
estremecidas de ranas.	quivering with frogs.
"Dios te salve" rezaremos	We will pray "God preserve you"
a Nuestra Señora de Agua	to Our Lady of Water
por la niña del estanque	for the girl of the pond
muerta bajo las manzanas.	dead beneath the apples.
Yo luego pondré a su lado	Then I'll place at her side
dos pequeñas calabazas	two small calabash gourds
para que se tenga a flote,	to keep her afloat,
¡ay! Sobre la mar salada.	oh! On the salty sea.

FROM GYPSY BALLADS

Gypsy Ballads offers a dramatic world in which gypsies act driven by love and hate, passion and remembrance, joy and sorrow. Their world centers on premonition and curse, on superstition and fright, a world that believes in the mortal curse of the moon and in the fatal curse of passion. Thirteen of the eighteen romances of the book end in pain, disillusion or death. Some readers took offense at the author's ruthless portrayal of the Civil Guard but others applauded it. For years Lorca had been haunted by images of the notorious police force. He perceived the Guard as an enemy of everything he stood for: poetry, song, art, life.

First *Gypsy Ballads*
1924 – 1927

Romance Sonámbulo – Sleepwalking Ballad

Verde que te quiero verde.	Green I want you green.
Verde viento. Verdes ramas.	Green wind. Green branches.
El barco sobre la mar	The boat on the sea
y el caballo en la montaña.	and the horse on the mountain.
Con la sombra en la cintura,	With shade at her waist,
ella sueña en su baranda,	she dreams at her railing,
verde carne, pelo verde,	green flesh, green hair,
con ojos de fría plata.	with eyes of cold silver.
Verde que te quiero verde.	Green I want you green.
Bajo la luna gitana,	Under the gypsy moon,
las cosas la están mirando	things are looking at her
y ella no puede mirarlas.	and she cannot look at them.

*

Verde que te quiero verde.	Green I want you green.
Grandes estrellas de escarcha	Large stars of frost
vienen con el pez de sombra	come with the shadowy fish
que abre el camino del alba.	that opens the road of dawn.
La Higuera frota su viento	The fig tree rubs its wind
con la lija de sus ramas,	with the sandpaper of its branches,
y el monte, gato garduño,	and the hill, a wild cat,
eriza sus pitas agrias.	bristles with its sour agave.
Pero ¿quién vendrá? ¿Y por dónde?...	But who will come? And, from where?...
Ella sigue en su baranda	She is still at her railing
verde carne, pelo verde,	green flesh, green hair,
soñando en la mar amarga.	dreaming of the bitter sea.

*

—*Compadre, quiero cambiar*
mi caballo por su casa,
mi montura por su espejo,
mi cuchillo por su manta.
Compadre, vengo sangrando,
desde los puertos de Cabra.
—*Si yo pudiera, mocito,*
este trato se cerraba.
Pero yo ya no soy yo,
ni mi casa es ya mi casa.
—*Compadre, quiero morir*
decentemente en mi cama.
De acero, si puede ser,
con las sábanas de Holanda.
¿No ves la herida que tengo
desde el pecho a la garganta?
—*Trescientas rosas morenas*
lleva tu pechera blanca.
Tu sangre rezuma y huele
alrededor de tu faja.
Pero yo ya no soy yo,
ni mi casa es ya mi casa.
—*Dejadme subir al menos*
hasta las altas barandas.
Barandales de la luna
por donde retumba el agua.

*

—Friend, I want to trade
my horse for your house,
my saddle for your mirror,
my knife for your blanket.
Friend, I come bleeding,
from de mountain passes of Cabra.
—If I could, young man,
I'd close this deal with you.
But I am no longer I,
and my house is no longer my house.
—Friend, I want to die
decently in my bed.
A steel one, if possible,
with chambray sheets.
Don't you see the wound I have
from my chest to my throat?
—Three hundred brown roses
cover your white shirt front.
Your blood oozes and smells
around your waist.
But I am no longer I,
and my house is no longer my house.
—Let me climb at least
up to the high railings.
Large railings of the moon
where the water rumbles.

*

Ya suben los dos compadres	Up the two friends climb
hacia las altas barandas.	up to the high railings.
Dejando un rastro de sangre.	Leaving behind a trail of blood.
Dejando un rastro de lágrimas.	Leaving behind a trail of tears.
Temblaban en los tejados	On the roofs trembled
farolillos de hojalata.	little tin lanterns.
Mil panderos de cristal	A thousand cristal tambourines
herían la madrugada.	wounding the dawn.

*

Verde que te quiero verde,	Green I want you green,
verde viento, verdes ramas.	green wind, green branches.
Los dos compadres subieron.	Up the two friends climbed.
El largo viento, dejaba	The long wind, was leaving
en la boca un raro gusto	a strange taste in their mouth
de hiel, de menta y de albahaca.	of bile, of mint and of basil.
—¡Compadre! ¿Dónde está, dime,	—Friend, where is she, tell me,
dónde está tu niña amarga?	where is your bitter girl?
—¡Cuántas veces te esperó!	—How often she awaited you!
¡Cuántas veces te esperara,	How often she waited,
cara fresca, negro pelo,	fresh face, black hair,
en esta verde baranda!	on this green railing!

*

Sobre el rostro del aljibe	Over the well's face
se mecía la gitana.	the gypsy girl was rocking.
Verde carne, pelo verde,	Green flesh, green hair,
con ojos de fría plata.	with eyes of cold silver.
Un carámbano de luna	An icicle of moon
la sostiene sobre el agua.	holds her over the water.
La noche se puso íntima	The night became as intimate

como una pequeña plaza.	as a village square.
Guardias civiles borrachos	Drunken Civil Guards
en la puerta golpeaban.	pounding on the door.
Verde que te quiero verde.	Green I want you green.
Verde viento. Verdes ramas.	Green wind. Green branches.
El barco sobre la mar.	The boat on the sea.
Y el caballo en la montaña.	And the horse on the mountain.

FROM POET IN NEW YORK

In this collection's best poems, facts blend with fiction, and language with emotion, to yield both a public indictment of urban society and a private cry of despair. In New York, Lorca sees human suffering which began to move him closer to a marxist analysis of the human condition. It is Lorca's stage as a super realist, a reaction against the abstract intellectualism of cubist writers. The work postulates a fantasy world with some ties to reality. The poet explores the world of the subconscious dealing with what is human and at the same time infrahuman. He sees the metropolis as a gigantic machine that negates nature and promotes artificiality. The subjects of his poems include Wall Street, Harlem, Brooklyn Bridge and a small Jewish Cemetery. He wrote the *Landscape of the Vomiting Multitude* as a poem about Coney Island's crowds at sunset describing the effect of alcoholic drinks sold in those prohibition days to people not able to afford to deal with reliable bootleggers.

Poet in New York
1929 – 1930

Paisaje de la multitude que vomita –
Landscape of the vomiting multitude
(*Anochecer en Coney Island* – Dusk at coney Island)

La mujer gorda venía delante	The fat woman came first
arrancando las raíces y mojando	tearing out roots and moistening
el pergamino de los tambores	the skin of the drums
La mujer gorda,	The fat woman,
que vuelve de revés los pulpos agonizantes.	who turns dying octopuses inside out.
La mujer gorda, enemiga de la luna,	The fat woman, enemy of the moon,
corría por las calles y los pisos	running in the streets and deserted
deshabitados	buildings
y dejaba por los rincones	and leaving in the corners
pequeñas calaveras de paloma	small pigeon skulls
y levantaba las furias de los	and stirring up the furies of last
banquetes de los siglos últimos	centuries
y llamaba al demonio del pan	and summoning the demon of bread
por las colinas del cielo barrido	through the hills of the swept sky
y filtraba un ansia de luz	and filtering a longing for light
en las circulaciones subterráneas.	in the subterranean spheres.
Son los cementerios. Lo sé. Son los	Their graveyards. I know. The
cementerios	graveyards
y el dolor de las cocinas enterradas	and the pain of kitchens buried
bajo la arena.	under the sand.
Son los muertos, los faisanes y las	They are the dead, the pheasants
manzanas de otra hora	and apples of another time
los que empujan en la garganta.	those that push in the throat.

Llegaban los rumores de la selva del vómito
con las mujeres vacías, con niños de cera caliente,
con árboles fermentados y camareros incansables
que sirven platos de sal bajo las arpas de saliva.
Sin remedio, hijo mío. !Vomita! No hay remedio.
No es el vómito de los húsares sobre los pechos de la prostitute,
ni el vómito del gato que se tragó una rana por descuido.
Son los muertos que arañan con sus manos de tierra
las puertas de pedernal donde se pudren nublos y postres.
La mujer gorda venía delante con las gentes de los barcos,
de las tabernas y de los jardines.
El vómito agitaba delicadamente sus tambores
entre algunas niñas de sangre
que pedían protección a la luna.
¡Ay de mí! ¡Ay de mí! ¡Ay de mí!
Esta mirada mía fue mía, pero ya no es mía.
Esta mirada que tiembla desnuda por el alcohol

Murmurings **from** the jungle of vomit arrived
with empty women, with children of warm wax,
with fermented trees and tireless waiters
serving dishes of salt beneath harps of saliva.
Hopelessly, my son. Vomit! Hopelessly.
It's not the vomit of hussars on the breasts of whores,
nor the vomit of a cat that carelessly swallowed a frog.
They are the dead who scratch with their hands of clay
on flint gates where clouds and desserts decay.
The fat woman came first with the crowds from the ships,
from taverns and gardens.
The vomit was delicately shaking its drums
among some little girls of blood
who begged the moon for protection.
Alas! Alas! Alas!
The look on my face was mine, but now isn't mine.
This look trembling naked by alcohol

<table>
<tr><td>

y despide barcos increíbles
por las anémonas de los muelles.
Me defiendo con esta mirada
que mana de las ondas
   por donde el alba no se atreve
Yo, poeta sin brazos, perdido
entre la multitud que vomita,
sin caballo efusivo que corte
los espesos musgos de mis sienes.
Pero la mujer gorda seguía delante
y la gente buscaba las
   farmacias
donde el amargo tópico se
   fija.
Sólo cuando izaron la bandera
   y llegaron los primeros canes
la ciudad entera se agolpó
   en las barandillas del embarcadero.

</td><td>

and launching incredible ships
through the anemones of the wharfs.
I defend myself with this look
that flows from waves
   where the dawn doesn't dare to go,
I, poet without arms, lost
in the vomiting multitude,
with no unrestrained horse to cut
the dense moss from my temples.
But the fat woman was still ahead
and the crowds kept looking for
   pharmacies
where the bitter topical can be
   found.
Only when the flag was hoisted
   and the first dogs arrived
did the entire city crowd together
   at the railings of the pier.

</td></tr>
</table>

FROM THE TAMARIT DIVAN

Tamarit gives voice to ideas and images that had absorbed Lorca since childhood. His using this form was part of a widespread revival of interest in Arab culture in the early 1930s in Spain. It consists of two blocks of poems, eleven 'gacelas,' an Arabic form dealing with love and death, and nine 'qasidas,' a pre-Islamic form of ode. The finished collection divides the twenty poems into two roughly equal sections based on traditional Middle Eastern verse forms. Like their ancient Persian counterparts, Lorca's work dwells principally on love, sex and death. The volume as a whole offers a profound meditation on the constant exchange between the living and the dead, between earth and the cosmos. The *Divan* is both more personal and more erotic than any collection Lorca had written to date. Many poems bear veiled allusions to homosexual love and suggest Lorca's growing desire to acknowledge and to celebrate his sexuality.

The Tamarit Divan
1931 – 1934

Casidas – Qasidas
(*Del herido por el agua* – About one wounded by water)

Quiero bajar al pozo	I want to go down to the well
quiero subir los muros de Granada	I want to climb the walls of Granada
para mirar el corazón pasado	to behold the heart pierced
por el punzón oscuro de las aguas.	by the dark awl of water.
El niño herido gemía	The wounded child was crying
con una corona de escarcha.	with a frosty crown
Estanques, aljibes y fuentes	Ponds, cisterns and fountains
levantaban al aire sus espadas.	raised their swords in the air.
¡Ay qué furia de amor, qué hiriente filo,	Oh, what a frenzy of love, how cutting the edge
qué nocturno rumor, qué muerte blanca!	what nocturnal rumor, what white death!
¡Qué desiertos de luz iban hundiendo	What luminous deserts were sinking
los arenales de la madrugada!	the sandy spots of dawn!
El niño estaba solo	The child was alone

con la ciudad dormida en la garganta.	with the city asleeep in his throat.
Un surtidor que viene de los	A water jetspring coming from
sueños	dreams
lo defiende del hambre de las algas.	protect him from hunger of algae.
El niño y su agonía, frente a frente,	The child and his agony, face to face,
eran dos verdes lluvias enlazadas.	were two green rains interlaced.
El niño se tendía por la	The child stretched out on the
tierra	ground
y su agonía se curvaba.	and his agony curved in the air.
Quiero bajar al pozo,	I want to go down to the well,
quiero morir mi muerte a bocanadas,	I want to die my death by mouthfuls,
quiero llenar mi corazón de musgo,	I want to fill my heart with moss,
para ver al herido por el agua.	to see the one wounded by the water.

Gacelas – Ghazals
(*Recuerdo de amor* – Memory of love)

No te lleves tu recuerdo.	Don't take your memory with you.
Déjalo solo en mi pecho,	Leave it alone in my breast,
temblor de blanco cerezo	a shudder of a white cherry tree
en el martirio de enero.	in January martyrdom.
Me separa de los muertos	A wall of bad dreams
un muro de malos sueños.	separates me from the dead.
Doy pena de lirio fresco	I show pain of fresh lily
para un corazón de yeso.	for a heart of plaster.
Toda la noche en el huerto	All night in the orchard
mis ojos, como dos perros.	my eyes like two dogs.

Toda la noche, comiendo
los membrillos de veneno.

All through the night, eating
quince of poison.

Algunas veces el viento
es un tulipán de miedo;

Sometimes the wind
is a tulip of fear;

es un tulipán enfermo,
la madrugada de invierno.

is a sick tulip,
in the winter dawn.

Un muro de malos sueños
me separa de los muertos.

A wall of bad dreams
separates me from the dead.

La hierba cubre en silencio
el valle gris de tu cuerpo.

The grass covers in silence
the gray valley of your body.

Por el arco del encuentro
la cicuta está creciendo.

In the arc of the meeting
hemlock is growing.

Pero deja tu recuerdo,
déjalo solo en mi pecho.

But leave your memory,
leave it alone in my breast.

FROM SIX GALICIAN POEMS

The collection of these poems written in Galician is a tribute to the landscape and language of Galicia. Written between 1932 and 1934, they were published in 1935. The poems were composed after Lorca travelled to the region in 1931.

Six Galician Poems
1935

Madrigal a cibdá de Santiago – Madrigal for the city of Santiago

Chove in Santiago	It rains in Santiago
meu doce amor.	my sweet love.
Camelia branca do ar	White camellia of the air
brila entebrecido o sol.	the gloomy sun shines.
Chove in Santiago	It rains in Santiago
na noite escura.	in the dark night.
Herbas de prata e sono	Grasses of silver and dream
cobren a valeira lúa.	cover the vacant moon.
Olla a choiva pol-a rúa,	Look at the rain in the street,
laio de pedra e cristal.	lament of stone and glass.
Olla no vento esvído	Look on the languishing wind
soma e cinza do teu mar.	shadow and ash of your sea.
Soma e cinza do teu mar,	Shadow and ash of your sea,
Santiago, lonxe do sol;	Santiago, far from the sun;
ágoa de mañán anterga	water of ancient morning
trema no meu corazón.	trembles in my heart.

FROM LAMENT FOR IGNACIO SÁNCHEZ MEJÍAS

By the end of October 1934, Lorca had written a poem in memory of the bullfighter. In the first part of his *Lament for Ignacio Sánchez Mejías,* Lorca insists on the elements of fatality that conspired against Ignacio the day of his goring and that the bullfighter knew from the moment he announced his return to the ring that his fate was sealed. The poem begins with the dramatic description of the struggle between life and death and then covers the human tragedy of the bullfighter in the event in which nature participates in the death.

Lament for Ignacio Sánchez Mejías
1935

La cogida y la muerte – The goring and the death

A las cinco de la tarde	At five in the afternoon.
Eran las cinco en punto de la tarde.	It was exactly five in the afternoon.
Un niño trajo la blanca sábana	A child brought the white sheet
a las cinco de la tarde.	at five in the afternoon.
Una espuerta de cal ya prevenida	A basket of lime standing ready
a las cinco de la tarde.	at five in the afternoon
Lo demás era muerte y solo muerte	Everything else was death, only death
a las cinco de la tarde	at five in the afternoon.
El viento se llevó los algodones	The wind carried away the cotton swabs
a las cinco de la tarde.	at five in the afternoon.
Y el óxido sembró cristal y níquel	Oxide sowed glass and nickel
a las cinco de la tarde.	at five in the afternoon.

Ya luchan la paloma y el leopardo	Now the dove battles with the leopard
a las cinco de la tarde.	at five in the afternoon.
Y un muslo con un asta desolada	And a thigh with a desolate horn
a las cinco de la tarde.	at five in the afternoon.
Comenzaron los sones de bordón	Now began the drums of a bass string
a las cinco de la tarde.	at five in the afternoon.
Las campanas de arsénico y el humo	The bells of arsenic and smoke
a las cinco de la tarde	at five in the afternoon.
En las esquinas grupos de silencio	Groups of silence on the corners
a las cinco de la tarde.	at five in the afternoon.
¡Y el toro solo corazón arriba!	And the bull alone with a lifted heart!
a las cinco de la tarde.	at five in the afternoon.
Cuando el sudor de nieve fue llegando	When sweat of snow began to arrive
a las cinco de la tarde,	at five in the afternoon,
cuando la plaza se cubrió de yodo	when the arena was drenched in iodine
a las cinco de la tarde,	at five in the afternoon,
la muerte puso huevos en la herida	death laid eggs in the wound
a las cinco de la tarde.	at five in the afternoon.
A las cinco de la tarde.	At five in the afternoon.
A las cinco en punto de la tarde.	At exactly five in the afternoon.

Un ataúd con ruedas es la cama	The bed is a coffin on wheels
a las cinco de la tarde.	at five in the afternoon.
Huesos y flautas suenan en su oído	Bones and flutes play in his ear
a las cinco de la tarde.	at five in the afternoon.
El toro ya mugía por su frente	The bull already bellowed at his forehead
a las cinco de la tarde.	at five in the afternoon.
El cuarto se irisaba de agonía	The room turned iridescent in his agony
a las cinco de la tarde.	at five in the afternoon.
A lo lejos ya viene la gangrena	The gangrene appears in the distance
a las cinco de la tarde.	at five in the afternoon.

Trompa de lirio por las verdes ingles	A lily horn in the green loins
a las cinco de la tarde.	at five in the afternoon.
Las heridas quemaban como soles	The wounds burned like suns
a las cinco de la tarde,	at five in the afternoon,
y el gentío rompía las ventanas	and the crowd was breaking the windows
a las cinco de la tarde.	at five in the afternoon.
A las cinco de la tarde.	At five in the afternoon
¡ay qué terribles cinco de la tarde!	Ah, that terrible five in the afternoon!
¡Eran las cinco en todos los relojes!	It was five by all the clocks!
¡Eran las cinco en sombra de la tarde!	It was five in the shade of the afternoon!

FROM SONNETS OF DARK LOVE

Sonetos del Amor Oscuro (Sonnets of Dark Love) was one of the last series of poems written by Federico García Lorca. Infused with themes of longing, desire, and forbidden love, the poems were written in 1935, inspired by Lorca's secret love affair with a 19-year-old. The poems remained unpublished until 1984, though unauthorized editions were released before that date.

Sonnets of Dark Love
1935

Soneto de la Dulce Queja – Sonnet of the Sweet Lament

No me dejes perder la maravilla	Don't let me lose the marvel
de tus ojos de estatua, ni el acento	of your eyes of statue or the accent
que de noche me pone en la mejilla	that by night places on my cheek
la solitaria rosa de tu aliento.	the solitary rose of your breath.

Tengo miedo de ser en esta orilla	I am afraid to be on this shore
tronco sin ramas; y lo que más siento	a trunk without limbs; and what I most regret
es no tener la flor, pulpa o arcilla	is not to have the flower, pulp or clay
para el gusano de mi sufrimiento.	for the worm of my suffering.
Si tú eres el tesoro oculto mío,	If you are my hidden treasure,
si eres mi cruz y mi dolor mojado,	if you are my cross and my wet sorrow,
si yo soy el perro de tu señorío,	if I am the dog of your dominion,
no me dejes perder lo que he ganado	do not let me lose what I have won
y decora las ramas de tu río	and adorn the waters of your river
con hojas de mi otoño enajenado.	with leaves of my distant autumn.

Federico García Lorca in 1936, year of his assassination.

EPILOGUE

It has been a troubling experience for me to write about Federico García Lorca and the Spanish Civil War period. Following the war, the Spanish government drew a veil of silence over events leading up to and resulting from it although there was no family that was not profoundly impacted, usually badly. The silence was enforced by fear – freedom of speech, of the press and the right to assemble were forbidden by law. We feared the law, the Civil Guard and the secret police. Ironically even after the dictator died and democracy was revived, the press flexed its unchained muscles but conversations among Spaniards rarely turn to the conflict. It's a painful subject, one Spaniards don't want to revisit; one whose ghosts, like that of now beloved Federico Garcia Lorca, haunt us.

I moved to the U.S. not long after Franco died and dealt with the culture shock of facing a 'free' society. I wasn't happy with all of its ramifications, but what did impress me was separation of church and state. Would Spain have had a civil war if that had been the case in my country? Who's to say? Clearly the separation is best for both entities: the state because diverse religious groups can live within the state following their own belief path without conflict, hopefully; and best for the religion because the perceived crimes of the government or general disdain for the governing group, cannot be blamed on the Church. I hope that the ideal of a free and open society, one that fosters creativity and innovation, remains intact, so that brilliant and unconventional men like Garcia Lorca will not have died in vain.

BIBLIOGRAPHY

Adams, Mildred, *García Lorca: Playwright and Poet*, New York, George Braziller, 1977.

Barea, Antonio, *Lorca: The Poet and His People*, New York, Cooper Square Publishers, 1973.

Díaz-Plaja, Guillermo, *Federico García Lorca*, Madrid, Espasa-Calpe, 1954.

Edwards, Gwynne, *Lorca: The Theater Beneath the Sand*, London, Marion Boyars, 1980.

García Lorca, Francisco, *In the Green Morning: Memories of Federico*, New York, A New Directions Book, 1986

Gibson, Ian, *The Death of Lorca*, Chicago, J. Philip O'Hara, 1973.

Gibson, Ian, *Federico García Lorca: A Life*, New York, Pantheon Books, 1989.

Maurer, Christopher, *Ed., Federico García Lorca: Collected Poems*, New York, Farrar, Strauss and Giroux, 1991.

Stainton, Leslie, *Lorca: A Dream of Life*, New York, Farrar, Straus and Giroux, 1999.

NOTES ABOUT LORCA'S CLOSEST CONTEMPORARIES

Aladrén Perojo, Emilio
Sculptor student who was a sentimental friend of Federico between 1925 and 1927.

Alberti Merello, Rafael
Poet and member of the Generation of '27. A close friend of Federico at the Residencia de Estudiantes. An active anti-fascist during the war, he went into exile in Paris, then to Buenos Aires until his return to Spain in 1977.

Azaña Díaz-Gallo, Manuel
President of the Spanish Second Republic. He died in exile in France in 1940.

Buñuel Portolés, Luis
Spanish surrealist film director and friend of García Lorca and Salvador Dalí at the Residencia de Estudiantes.

Cummings, Philip
American friend of Lorca who invited him to spend time in a cabin in Vermont in the summer of 1929.

Dalí y Doménech, Salvador
Close friend of Federico at the Residencia de Estudiantes and thereafter. He was a universally known surrealist painter, sculptor and writer.

De Falla, Manuel
Spanish composer. He had a strong influence on the Generation of '27, including on Federico García Lorca. He was a close friend of the poet.

De los Ríos Urruti, Fernando
Socialist university professor who influenced Federico's liberal views. After the war, he went into exile in New York where he died in 1949. His daughter Laura married Lorca's brother Francisco.

De Onís Sánchez, Sánchez
Philologist, Professor at Residencia de Estudiantes, Madrid, and Columbia University who facilitated Lorca's stay in New York.

Díaz Artigas, Josefina
Argentinian artist performer of the premiere of Lorca's *Blood Wedding.*

Domínguez Berrueta, Martín

Professor at the University of Granada. Teacher of Federico García Lorca who organized study trips around the country for his students. He stimulated Federico's interest in the Arts.

Fernández-Montesinos Lustau, Manuel

Mayor of Granada in 1936 who was married to Federico's sister Concha. He was assassinated by the rebels on August 16 accused of being a socialist militant.

Franco Bahamonde, Francisco

Dictator of Spain from 1936 to 1975. One of the conspirators who initiated the Spanish Civil War. Nearly 400,000 Spaniards went into exile abroad at the end of the conflict.

García Lorca, Concepción (Concha)

Sister of Federico. She married Manuel Fernández-Montesinos, mayor of Granada assassinated by the nationalist rebels.

García Lorca, Francisco

Brother of Federico four years younger than the poet. A diplomat and literary historian. After the Spanish Civil War, he went into exile in the United States where he became a professor at Columbia University.

García Lorca, Isabel

Youngest sister of Federico. Writer and university literature professor.

García Rodríguez, Don Federico
Father of the poet. A wealthy landowner of Fuente Vaqueros in the Vega near Granada. At the end of the war, he went into exile in New York where he died in 1945.

Gil-Robles y Quiñones, José María
Spanish politician co-founder of CEDA, a Catholic right-wing political party.

Larsen, Nella
American novelist who introduced Federico to the black community in Harlem.

Lorca Romero, Doña Vicenta
Mother of Federico. A quiet local school mistress daughter of an agricultural worker.

Loynaz Muñoz, Dulce María
Cuban writer who hosted Federico during his stay in Havana.

Machado Ruiz, Antonio
Romantic Spanish poet, friend of Federico from the year they met in Baeza when García Lorca was a student at the University of Granada. He fled Spain when Franco's army was approaching Barcelona and died in Colliure, France in February, 1939.

Membrives Fernández, Lola
Argentinian actress performer of Lorca's *Blood Wedding* and other plays.

Neruda, Pablo
Poet, socialist politician from Chile. He was a good friend of García Lorca.

Primo de Rivera, José Antonio
Spanish politician founder of the fascist party Falange Española.

Rivas Cherif, Cipriano
Theater director who helped Lorca produce his plays.

Rodríguez Rapún, Rafael
Secretary of La Barraca and sentimental friend of Lorca's.

Rosales Camacho, Luis
Poet, friend of Federico who hid him in his house in Granada to avoid incarceration.

Ruiz Alonso, Ramón
Activist in Granada during the uprising against the republic. He wrote the accusation against Lorca denouncing him as leftish and anti-Catholic.

Sánchez Mejías, Ignacio
Spanish bullfighter whose death in the arena inspired Lorca to write his *Llanto por Ignacio Sánchez Mejías* in 1935.

Valdés Guzmán, José
As civil governor of Granada, he is believed to have been the military commander who issued the order to assassinate Federico García Lorca without a trial.

Xirgu Subirá, Margarita

Theater actress associated with Lorca's plays. Exiled after the war, she adopted Uruguayan citizenship. She died in Montevideo in 1969.